MARCO ⊕ POLO

KRA KOW

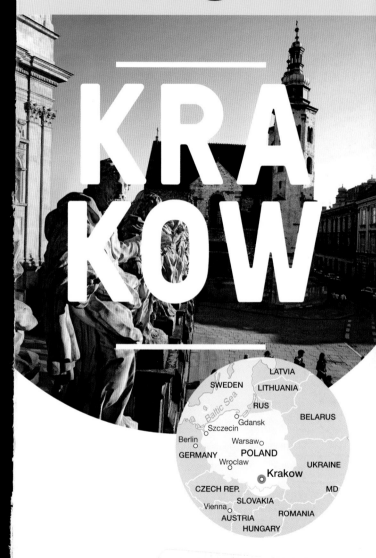

LATVIA

SWEDEN · LITHUANIA

Baltic Sea · RUS

Gdansk · BELARUS

Szczecin

Berlin · Warsaw

GERMANY · POLAND

Wroclaw · UKRAINE

Krakow

CZECH REP. · MD

SLOVAKIA

Vienna

AUSTRIA · ROMANIA

HUNGARY

T0150576

THE TOURING APP

shows you the way...
including routes and offline maps!

GET MORE OUT OF YOUR MARCO POLO GUIDE

IT'S AS SIMPLE AS THIS

1 go.marco-polo.com/kra

2 download and discover

GO!

WORKS OFFLINE!

SYMBOLS

INSIDER TIP	Insider Tip
★	Highlight
●●●●	Best of...
☀	Scenic view
♻	Responsible travel: for ecological or fair trade aspects
(*)	Telephone numbers that are not toll-free

PRICE CATEGORIES HOTELS

Expensive	over 550 złoty
Moderate	250–550 złoty
Budget	under 250 złoty

Prices are valid per night for two people in a double room with breakfast

PRICE CATEGORIES RESTAURANTS

Expensive	over 75 złoty
Moderate	40–75 złoty
Budget	under 40 złoty

Prices are valid for a meal with starter, main course and dessert without drinks

On the cover: Underground Market Square Museum p. 34 | Trendy Kazimierz district p. 42

DID YOU KNOW?
Krakow's artistic duo → p. 23
Fit in the city → p. 36
Local specialities → p. 56
Favourite eateries → p. 58
Time to chill → p. 71
More than a good night's sleep → p. 78
Public holidays → p. 97
Budgeting → p. 103
For bookworms & film buffs → p. 102
Weather in Krakow → p. 104
Currency converter → p. 105

MAPS IN THE GUIDEBOOK
(112 A1) Page numbers and coordinates refer to the street atlas
(0) Site/address located off the map
Coordinates are also given for places not marked on the street atlas

(*m̈ A–B 2–3*) Refers to the removable pull-out map

INSIDE FRONT COVER:
The best highlights

INSIDE BACK COVER:
Public transport map

The best MARCO POLO Insider Tips

Our top 15 Insider Tips

INSIDER TIP **Modest beauty**
Although it's often overshadowed by Krakow's more well-known churches, the baroque *Church of St Anne* boasts an elaborate interior design and is one of the most magnificent 18th-century buildings Poland has to offer → p. 32

INSIDER TIP **Creative with pizza**
At *Pizzatopia*, the bakers let their pizza dough rise for 48 hours before they let visitors create their own masterpieces. The art takes just three minutes to bake and is always served crispy → p. 55

INSIDER TIP **Up for some opera?**
While in Krakow, you should pay at least one visit to the *Opera Krakowska*. To avoid letting yourself down, make sure you book your tickets in advance → p. 73

INSIDER TIP **Artist with a green thumb**
The garden behind the *Józef Mehoffer House* serves as a tranquil refuge in this bustling city → p. 46

INSIDER TIP **A journey back in time**
Observing the impressive photographs displayed at the *Galician Museum* will take you back to the long-forgotten world of the Galician Jews → p. 43

INSIDER TIP **Seek and find**
The *flea market on Plac Nowy* is a real treasure trove, regardless of whether you are looking for a Prada bag and other designer articles at reasonable prices or Jewish candelabras made of silver → p. 43

INSIDER TIP **Where extras are all part of the service**
Hotel Royal at the foot of Wawel Hill offers beautiful and affordable accommodation just a stroll away from the castle and the cathedral → p. 81

INSIDER TIP **Royal setting**
The *Wawel Evenings* are very special: enjoy the summer concerts and opera in the castle's arcaded courtyard → p. 73

BEST OF...

GREAT PLACES FOR FREE
Discover new places and save money

● *History lessons in the royal basilica*
Although the Wawel Cathedral is one of Poland's biggest attractions, many parts of its lavishly decorated interior are free for visitors to enter (photo) → p. 37

● *Party – without limits*
For those who want to dance the night away in Krakow and are full of energy, most clubs don't charge an admission fee after 1am → p. 72

● *A treat for your ears*
Enjoy a free concert in an environment made for classical music. Many *Krakow churches* put on incredible live music events and don't charge a penny to attend → p. 33

● *Art under a canopy of leaves*
It is hard to imagine a more beautiful site for a sculpture exhibition. Stroll through the *Planty*, the strip of parkland surrounding the Old Town, and admire one of the largest collections of 19th and 20th-century monuments → p. 33

● *Museums are free on Sundays or Mondays*
Whether it is the *Józef Mehoffer House,* the *National Museum* or the *Archaeological Museum on the Wawel*, you can visit many permanent exhibitions on Sundays or Mondays without having to pay → p. 33

● *A new panoramic view of the city*
Although the lookout points over Krakow usually require an entrance fee, in Podgórze on top of *Krakus Mound*, you'll have a free panoramic view overlooking the beautiful Vistula River → p. 24

● *A free visit to the Museum of Modern Art*
Every Tuesday at the *MOCAK*, you can experience fascinating modern art for absolutely nothing! However, if you decide to go, make sure you get in the queue early since the free tickets are a hot commodity and tend to go fairly quickly → p. 46

●●●● Dots in guidebook refer to 'Best of...' tips

ONLY IN KRAKOW
Unique experiences

● *The dancing, fire-breathing dragon*
The legend lives on: the dragon from the medieval saga can be seen everywhere in the city and is at the heart of the annual *Dragon Parade* in June, a celebration with many concerts and family picnics on the Vistula River → p. 96

● *In the astronomer's study*
Poland's oldest university had already been operating for 130 years when Nicolaus Copernicus started his studies at the *Collegium Maius*. Touring its magnificent chambers is an experience that will take you back through time → p. 30

● *In the heart of town*
The *Rynek Główny* is not only the largest Gothic square in Europe but also one of the most beautiful. Climb up the *Town Hall Tower* and be charmed by the unique expanse and architecture of the Market Square down below → p. 33, 35

● *Live international jazz music*
Krakow is a jazz city and the stars perform in the fabulous brick-wall setting of an old cellar in *Harris Piano Jazz Bar* – you can recharge your batteries with the good music and drinks served there! (photo) → p. 70

● *The sunken world of medieval Krakow*
You can really delve deep into the history of the city at the *Rynek Podziemny (Rynek Underground)*. Located beneath Cloth Hall, this museum takes visitors through a mysteriously illuminated, detailed reconstruction of medieval Krakow → p. 35

● *Synagogues and the sound of klezmer*
In Kazimierz, you'll experience Jewish history and culture like never before. At *Klezmer Hois*, you'll enjoy an evening of Jewish food and the swinging sounds of klezmer music, a genre combining many musical styles → p. 58

● *What the academic does at night*
For more than 700 years, Krakow students have been working hard at their studies. At night, however, they hit the clubs to forget about everything. *Pod Jaszczurami* is one of the city's oldest nightclubs, and they've been throwing wild parties since the 1960s → p. 69

ONLY IN

BEST OF...

● *Visit a true animal lover and lady*
She's been doing a lot of travelling in recent years, but the 'Lady with an Ermine' can now be seen at the National Museum, so take your time while visiting this famous painting by Leonardo da Vinci → p. 47

● *Be scandalous, relax!*
If it's pouring outside to the point of discomfort, head over to *Le Scandale* for breakfast and spend the entire day relaxing with a good book and waiting for the sun's return → p. 72

● *Discover a new hobby*
Vibrant rays of light bursting through leadlights – this Krakow symbol is best experienced at the *Stained Glass Museum*. Turn a rainy day into an adventure by taking a course on how to make one of these beautiful glass treasures yourself → p. 47

● *Follow the red brick road*
The original brick architecture was integrated into the modern construction of the *Galeria Kazimierz* shopping centre. This special charm, as well as the cinemas, restaurants, cafés and a play area for children, makes this one of the most pleasant places to go shopping → p. 62

● *Through the hard war years*
In *Oskar Schindler's former enamelware factory*, you will be able to learn about the indescribable suffering experienced by the Jewish and non-Jewish population during the Nazi occupation. You should allow yourself plenty of time for this moving experience (photo) → p. 46

● *Soaking wet but doing fine*
Don't let some dreary weather ruin your day! The spirit of summer is always alive at *Aqua Park Cracow*. This indoor amusement park allows the kids to shoot down water slides while mum and dad spend the day doing yoga or relaxing in the sauna → p. 94

RAIN

RELAX AND CHILL OUT
Take it easy and spoil yourself

● *Watching the flowers grow*
The *Botanical Gardens* cover an impressive 25 acres. Sitting near the small lake on a warm day, reading a good book or just watching the flowers grow, is heaven. What more could you wish for? (photo) → **p. 48**

● *Invigorate weary limbs*
One-of-a-kind amber massages, the oriental art of relaxation, chocolate peelings: recharge your batteries in style between the handmade furniture from Bali in the *Farmona Wellness & Spa* → **p. 71**

● *Just dream away*
At the *ARS Krakow Cinema Center*, you'll sink into big, comfy armchairs and surround yourself with old-fashioned cinema lighting. This cinema offers five splendidly antiquated screening rooms and a laid-back environment. → **p. 71**

● *Intoxicating views at dinner*
An evening meal in the time-honoured *Wentzl Restaurant* is a feast for the senses in itself. But with the view of the Rynek Główny and illuminated St Mary's Church thrown in, the pleasure is absolutely perfect → **p. 57**

● *Don't forget your swimming gear!*
Why not combine your city break with an element of a beach holiday? The artificial *Kryspinów Lake* just outside Krakow offers all kinds of relaxing summer activities → **p. 71**

● *A coffee and a book, please*
Sit back, have a cup of coffee, browse through novels, look at illustrated books and just enjoy the calm at the relaxing bookstore and café *De Revolutionibus* → **p. 61**

● *Swaying gently*
The city drifts slowly past you while a gentle breeze wafts over the railing. This beautiful *boat trip on the Vistula* offers an ideal alternative to your otherwise run-of-the-mill city sightseeing tour → **p. 105**

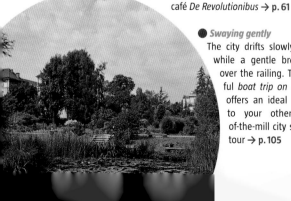

DISCOVER KRAKOW!

Krakow's centuries-old, rich and eventful history is plain for all to see, but visitors to the city will find no trace of the stuffy museum-like atmosphere experienced elsewhere. The metropolis on the Vistula River is *full of energy and exudes an almost southern joie de vivre*. The city appears to be charmed in more than one respect. It was protected from destruction by invading armies and enemy forces for centuries and became *one of the most important centres of scholarship in Europe* in the 14th and 15th centuries. This has all helped make the gem on the Vistula *the most visited city in Poland*. Krakow's unique atmosphere – a mixture of culture and vitality, of history and modernity, of the future and past legend – draws a growing number of visitors each year to walk in Copernicus's footsteps, take part in festivals and take a journey through time in the midst of immortal architecture. Or they simply come to enjoy life in the restaurants, cafés and clubs that are on a par with those in larger metropolises. Krakow has a big heart; in fact it is one of the world's largest: the *Rynek Główny*, the main square in the centre of the Old Town measures 220 × 220 yd – an open space which itself makes a huge impression amidst the sea of houses arranged with the regularity of a chessboard around it. Krakow's heart is surrounded by absolute beauty, by houses and other buildings of *every conceivable architectural style* and period. The metropolis on the Vistula has managed to survive the last 800 years *more or less unscathed*. It is also anything but a museum: city life centres around this square, this is where the people from Krakow meet, this is where the action is – and that until late at night and deep under the ground.

> **Krakow really starts to buzz on summer evenings**

Many of the more than 100 cafés, restaurants, bars and clubs around Rynek Główny that get Krakow's nightlife into full swing – especially on warm summer evenings – are located *in traditional brick vaults* below street level. The city's lifelines go deep. As in many old metropolises, street levels change as the centuries progress, due to earth deposits and layers of construction work – ground floors sink to cellar level. You can get a startling insight into what this subterranean world looks like at the *Rynek Underground Museum* (see p. 35). Or simply by drinking a beer in one of the historic beer cellars: take your cue from the local residents. They love going out – the bars are full whatever the time of day. There is a common saying that 'People work in Warsaw but live in Krakow.'

Krakow had a hard time getting over the fact that the royal court moved to its unloved sister, which then became the capital, 400 years ago. However, the city compensated for its fall into relative unimportance in its own way: it became a magical city, the protector of stories and legends, the patron of poets, musicians and painters. The fact that Krakow is considered to be Poland's cultural capital is not only due to the splendour of its architectural monuments, which led to the entire centre

Live like a local. These sun seekers head to Plac Nowy to soak it in!

being named a Unesco World Heritage Site. Its reputation is further supported by the large number of *theatres, concert halls, galleries and museums* to be found in what – with a population of 770,000 – is a relatively small city. In addition, there is a *jazz scene* that connoisseurs consider comparable only with New York. Many *world-famous artists*, including film director and Oscar prizewinner An-

Poland's cultural capital and its treasures

drzej Wajda and composer Krzysztof Penderecki, one of the leading Polish avant-garde musicians, live and work in Krakow or have done in the past. Poet and winner of the Nobel Prize for Literature, Wisława Szymborska, did not live to see Krakow being named *Unesco City of Literature* in 2003. She spent practically her whole life in the city on the Vistula and died in February 2012. Similarly, Czesław Miłosz, who was also awarded the Nobel Prize for Literature, lived and died – after his time in exile – in Krakow. We should also not forget *klezmer music*, the traditional Jewish folk music, which is as vibrant as ever and underlines Krakow's importance as a *former centre of Jewish life in Europe*.

Krakow's Jewish heritage is concentrated in *Kazimierz*; the formerly independent town was incorporated in 1800. Expelled from Krakow in 1495 by the then king following a series of pogroms, many Jews settled in Kazimierz and it developed into an important centre of their culture. The *peaceful coexistence* with the Catholic neighbours lasted until the German occupation of Poland in 1939. Only around 5000 of the 60,000 Jews living in Kazimierz survived the Nazi horror. Director Steven Spielberg paid tribute to the suffering of Krakow's Jews – in 1939, they were 25% of the population – and the industrialist Oskar Schindler, who saved more than 1100 forced la-

bourers from being murdered, in his *film 'Schindler's List'*. Today, Kazimierz has managed to preserve its unique flair; one in which the happy times of the past have come to life again: at the end of June and early in July, the Festival of Jewish Culture, probably Krakow's most important festival, is held in Kazimierz. It is a *youthful, hip district*, popular with students and artists, an in-place for night owls and party-goers, who have fun all night in summer and *hunt for retro chic at the flea markets*.

Centuries-old Krakow emanates a feeling of youthful freshness. The *more than 200,000 students* make it a young city and its dynamic development can also be seen in the establishment of state and private universities. They have taken their place alongside the *oldest university in Poland* and one of the oldest in the world: it was founded in 1364. Wawel Hill, with Wawel Royal Castle and Wawel Cathedral – which are tourist highlights – was settled more than 50,000 years ago. There is proof that salt mining was carried out near Krakow starting around 1400 BC.

Lectures and lessons – Krakow has been a university town since 1364

Krakow was first mentioned in a document in 965, indicating that the settlement on Wawel Hill had developed into an important trading centre at the *intersection of a number of major trade routes*. Krakow grew, became an episcopal see and capital city and also had to survive devastating strikes by the Tatars in the 13th century. The trumpet call that can be heard every hour from the tower of St Mary's Church recalls these attacks: the *Hejnał* then stops abruptly, a reminder that the lookout was hit by an arrow while

Where Nicolaus Copernicus learned the science of astronomy: Collegium Maius

he was blowing his warning – and another example of how far back Krakow's history reaches and how it still has its place in present-day life. This trumpet call is also transmitted live throughout Poland on the radio at midday. Krakow experienced its heyday in the 15th and 16th centuries, which is clearly visible in the *magnificent Renaissance architecture*. The city attracted artists, progressive thinkers and scholars. Nicolaus Copernicus, who would later create a new view of the universe, was just one of the many who studied at Krakow University. There are more than 400 sights within the Planty, a *green belt encircling the Old Town*. These include townhouses, palaces, famous museums with collections of international and Polish art and, last but not least, *17 churches*. The number of houses of worship funded by monarchs, the nobility and other rich citizens provides striking evidence of the city's wealth. The world-famous treasures in the churches, such as the altarpiece created by the sculptor Veit Stoss for St Mary's Church, attract art lovers and pilgrims alike.

Krakow has always been a centre of religious life in Poland. In the past, the city played a significant role as a *diocese and site of the coronation of the country's kings*. Krakow is often called a 'papal city', although Karol Wojtyła, the later *Pope John Paul II*, was not born here (he actually came from Wadowice). Nonetheless, Wojtyła spent more than 40 years in Krakow and left an indelible mark on the city. Destined to become the Archbishop of Krakow, this man opposed those in power during the Nazi occupation by studying theology although it was forbidden. No matter the weather, he later celebrated open-air Masses to protest against the anticlerical socialist regime which in post-war Poland prohibited workers from building a church in Nowa Huta. One year before being elected Pope, however, his fight and the workers' opposition finally paid off. Karol Wojtyła consecrated the 'Ark of the Lord' Church in Nowa Huta.

Krakow and *socialism* is an interesting consideration in itself, and it is hard to imagine two more opposing mindsets. On the one hand, you have the city of liberals, freethinkers and dissenters. On the other, you have the regime, a regime

> **Centre of religious life in Poland**

that saw no place for these bourgeois tendencies in their classless society. To take the wind out of the sails of bourgeois resistance, those in power quickly built the district of Nowa Huta and a steel mill to go along with it. In doing so, they hoped to create a settlement for proletarian workers. Their plans backfired, however, and the complete opposite happened. It was precisely these workers and their strong adherence to the Catholic Church that finally brought about the collapse of the system.

Today, the steel plant is a thing of the past. The people living here have come to terms with the upheaval caused by the end of socialism and the opening up of the country in the 1990s. Today, Krakow lives off tourism, its service sector and its university. The city is the largest employer in the region and for years now, Krakow has been able to boast the lowest unemployment rate they've ever had – it's currently less than 4% and far below the national average. An increasing number of visitors come to Krakow to pay their respects to *Leonardo da Vinci's 'Lady with an Ermine'*, admire the Cloth Hall in the Market Square, stroll through Nowa Huta and see Kazimierz. Almost 13 million tourists come here each year. Krakow's inhabitants are fully aware that they live in a very special city – and they are proud of the fact. They love and cultivate its history and traditions and know how to celebrate these for days on end – no matter whether the festivities are religious or of a more worldly nature. It is also said that the locals are thrifty, if not downright stingy. That may well be true, but they are also *hospitable and cosmopolitan*. That is why some people, including the violinist Nigel Kennedy, fall so deeply in love with the city that they choose to stay, live and work there – and thus write their own contribution to the further chapters of Krakow's eternal history.

WHAT'S HOT

1 Around the clock

Pubs and bars If you're needing a late night snack, Krakow has got you covered – the pubs are open almost 24/7! *Pijalnia Wódki i Piwa* has four locations *(e.g. Ulica Szewska 20)* and is open daily from 9am to 6am *(photo)*. Along with snacks, they offer cheap vodka and beer. A more stylish (but no less delicious) place is *Ambasada Śledzia (daily 9am–midnight | Ulica Stolarska 8/10)*. Serving only Polish cuisine, *Gospoda Koko (Ulica Gołębia 8 | www.gospoda koko.pl)* is open daily 8am–3am.

Old made new

2

Urban jewels Located in Krakow's former slaughterhouse, the *Galeria Kazimierz* (see p. 62) *(photo)* is one of the most beautiful examples that shows how the city has modernised the functions of many of its old structures. Another example is the *Forum Designu (Mon–Sat 11am–7pm, Sun until 5pm | Ulica Focha 1)*. Offering an impressive range of furniture and accessories made by local designers, the store's on the ground floor of the Cracovia Hotel, which dates back to the Soviet era. Once a former tobacco factory, *Tytano (Dolnych Młynów 10)* is a massive, renovated complex offering alternative shops and hip bars similar to those in New York and Berlin.

3 Coffee with culture

Artistic delights Changing photographic exhibitions await you at *Café Młynek (Plac Wolnica 7)*, while *Café Cheder (Ulica Józefa 36 | www.jewishfestival.pl)* not only has Israeli coffee and Moroccan tea with mint leaves but also a selection of books (also in English) on Jewish history and culture. The colourfully decorated *Massolit Books & Café (Ulica Felicjanek 4) (photo)* boasts a substantial English-language library.

An outdoor feast

Street food In the summer months, it's typical to see people enjoying life on Krakow's streets both day and night. Today, street food is also becoming more and more common. Especially in *Kazimierz*, you'll see entire streets lined with street food. These include *Ulica św. Wawrzyńca, Ulica Dajwór* and *Ulica Mostowa*. The squares *Nowy* and *Wolnica* are also an oasis for street food. Whether at these locations, on the *Ulica Lipowa* in *Podgórze* or in the district of *Grzegórzki*, you'll find colourfully lit courtyards covered with deck chairs. Some of the food offered includes burgers, fries, pancakes and the original Krakow bagel that Polish emigrants imported to the USA.

Drink local

Beer and wine Unique environments and delicious brew. More and more small breweries are starting to offer their beer on tap. Located in one of the city's many beautiful cellars, the mini-brewery *C. K. Browar (daily from 9am | Podwale 6–7 | ckbrowar.pl)* also offers tasty Polish cuisine. The brewery *Stara Zajezdnia (Mon–Fri 2pm–11pm, Sat midday–midnight, Sun midday–10pm | Ulica św. Wawrzyńca 12 | www.stara zajezdniakrakow. pl)* was once a former tram depot. The interior boasts a unique industrial style, and many flock here for their homemade brew. In summer, you can relax outside on one of the courtyard's many deck chairs. Polish wine is also popular here. Sample house wine at *Krako Slow Wines (daily from 10am | Ulica Lipowa 6f | krako slowwines.pl)* or at *Stoccaggio (Mon–Sat from 11am, Sun from 2pm | Ulica Krupnicza 9/2 | stoccaggio.pl)*. Even the university has a vineyard! Their wine can be bought in the café located in the *Collegium Maius*.

IN A NUTSHELL

A WORLD OF READING

If you're walking through Planty Park and see someone on a bench with a smartphone to their ear, it doesn't necessarily mean they're talking on their phone. They may very well be listening to a Nobel Prize winner. Ever since 2013 when Krakow became one of Unesco's cities of literature, the city has turned dozens of park benches into audio books. Anyone who scans the QR code on the backrest will receive information on the life and work of Nobel Laureates of Literature. These include Wisława Szymborska, Czesław Miłosz (both of whom live in Krakow), and many other writers and authors. You'll find these benches not only in Planty Park, but also in Kazimierz and Nowa Huta. Visit *kody.*

miastoliteratury.pl to find an interactive map indicating at least 180 literary park benches, cafés, bookshops and other places related to literature and reading. Those who love books will also be impressed with Krakow. The first bookshop in Europe opened here in 1610! Today, the city offers around 80 bookstores and almost 30 second-hand bookshops for reading fans to indulge in. In addition to two literature festivals, Krakow also hosts the country's largest international book fair. Visit *krakowcityofliterature.com* for more information.

A T THE COFFEE HOUSE

Sitting in a coffee house is not only a must in Krakow but also a way to travel back in time. These time machines not

Photo: Fountain on Rynek Główny

On art and legends, jazz and klezmer, kings and popes, princesses and dragons – and the magic of a city

only take you to the Middle Ages; you can also head back to the 19th century when Krakow was occupied by Austria. All it takes is letting the environment of a wonderfully nostalgic coffeehouse immerse your senses. Cafés like *Kawiarnia Noworolski* (see p. 54) or *Kawiarnia Europejska* feel just as authentic as *Hawełka* (see p. 57), a restaurant that the city calls the 'Purveyor to the Imperial and Royal Court'. The horse-drawn carriages on the Market Square are reminiscent of Vienna, the city that inspired Krakow's art and

architecture in the 19th century. The impact was so great that even the restaurant *Pod Złotą Pipą (Ulica Floriańska 30)* placed the Austrian Emperor Franz Josef on their sign. Today, he watches over the guests as they enjoy their meals in the restaurant's Gothic cellar.

All these locations take you back to a time when Krakow belonged to Galicia, a time when the city was part of the Kingdom of Galicia and Lodomeria. The kingdom included the Grand Duchy of Krakow, the Duchy of Zator and the Duchy

Krakow has jazz in its veins; no day goes by without at least one exciting concert

of Auschwitz. Today, the former region of Galicia belongs to Ukraine and Poland, which were both parts of the Habsburg Monarchy between 1772 and 1918. This was an economically hard time for the city on the Vistula. Culturally speaking, however, the province enjoyed its freedom. Art, cabaret, Polish theatre and literature were all flourishing.

BOOMTOWN

If you've ever wondered if the increasing number of vegan and vegetarian restaurants in a city has anything to do with its air quality, Krakow has the answer – yes, it does. For years, the city has been attracting tech and service companies from all over the world, and it's created a booming economy here. All over Europe, members of the young and well-educated 'Google Generation' are moving to the city on the Vistula. More and more foreign students are also coming here. From 2006 to 2017, the numbers rose from 10,000 to 65,000, and a total of 210,000 young people attend the universities in Krakow. The city is vibrating with energy. The districts of Zabłocie, where a modern dormitory for 1000 students is currently being built, and Podgórze are all the rage. Galleries, bars, clubs, lofts and even vegan or vegetarian restaurants are springing up everywhere. Because of the economic boom, Krakow is up there with cities like Paris or Berlin, but this is making the city more expensive, and the increased traffic is having an effect on the city's air quality. Luckily, the city has recognised the problem and is taking measures against the smog.

DANCE THE KLEZMER

If it's not jazz being played in Krakow, it must be klezmer. It's not as hip as the jazz coming from America, but it is a lot older. The first texts mentioning the *klezmorim* (i.e. travelling musicians who play traditional Jewish music) date from the 15th century. Weddings and harvest festivals wouldn't be the same without them and their cheerful dance music. Later, klezmer was influenced by the music played at Ashkenazi Jewish weddings in Eastern Europe and mixed with joyous Ukrainian, Russian, and Bulgarian music of the Sinti and Roma. Klezmer was then brought to the US by Eastern-European Jewish emigrants where it developed further. It was especially popular at the beginning of the 20th century and from there, the genre took on a new form. Today, the music's evolution has long since matured, but some musicians create new styles by combining it with jazz.

In both Poland and Krakow, many young bands like *Kroke (www.kroke.krakow.pl)* and *Nazar* are following in their ancestors' footsteps and even play the traditional, klezmer instruments (i.e. clarinet, violin and drums). You'll hear them in the synagogues, restaurants, the *Galicia Jewish Museum*, *Klezmer-Hois*, the *Klezmer Music Venue (Sławkowska 14 |* *cracowconcerts.com/klezmer-music)* and during the Jewish Culture Festival.

LEGENDS GALORE!

Keep in mind: it's rarely a good idea to have lamb stuffed with sulphur, tar and pepper for lunch. As unusual as this meal may sound, it played an important role in Krakow's most famous (but not only) fairy tale. The story's bad guy is a cave-dwelling dragon at the foot of *Wawel Hill*. In the story, he feeds off the city's virgins sacrificed to him. This changes, however, when a brave cobbler comes and serves him this unusually stuffed lamb. In eating it, the fire-breathing dragon gets an unbearably upset stomach. He drinks from the Vistula to soothe the pain, but he ends up drinking himself to the point of combustion. It's a rather unappetizing meal, but in the end, it won the cobbler the princess's hand in marriage! Despite his bravery, the city gave the dragon the true fame and glory – on the Market Square, you can buy stuffed animals of him at every stand and

KRAKOW'S ARTISTIC DUO

Two great artists left their mark on Krakow at completely different times; one in the 15th and the other in the 19th century. Veit Stoss came to Krakow from Nuremberg in 1477. It is not really known where the sculptor and painter learned his art nor which works he created before leaving Nuremberg. He became famous with his monumental main altar for St Mary's Church. The 13-m/43-ft-high and 11-m/36-ft-wide altar is considered one of the great masterpieces of Gothic carving. After 19 years in Krakow, he left the city as a highly respected citizen and returned to Nuremberg where he created many other masterpieces before his death in 1533.

The main artistic personality of the fin-de-siècle in the 19th century was Stanisław Wyspiański, a man who could turn his hand to many things, who studied in Paris and made a name for himself as a painter and writer. He also designed furniture and complete interiors, the sets for his plays, and glass windows including those in the Franciscan Church. Nature, simple peasant life and Polish history are the leitmotifs of his creative work.

in summer, colourful depictions of him parade through the city.

Krakow is a city full of myths, fairy tales and legends. The pigeons on Rynek Główny, for example, are said to have once been knights so no one ever dares to drive them away. They say a witch turned them into birds after their master failed to pay her back the money she lent him. Then there's the trumpet call. In memory of the 13th-century Mongol Invasion of Poland, it can be heard on the hour from St Mary's Church. At midday, the sound is even broadcast on national radio. Next, we have the *Lajkonik*, a man dressed in Mongol attire and who also symbolises the invasion. In summer, he walks across the marketplace trying to touch everyone with his sceptre. Let him – it's said to bring good luck!

LOW-KEY OR PUNK-LIKE

A butterfly. A black star. Krakow. They all have one thing in common: jazz music. Without it, Kendrick Lamar's hip-hop masterpiece 'To Pimp a Butterfly', David Bowie's final studio album 'Blackstar' and the city on the Vistula would all be without a heart. In Krakow, the capital of Polish jazz, whether you're in a café, restaurant or club, it seems you hear jazz music everywhere. The first real jazz bands began playing here almost 100 years ago and little has changed ever since. Jazz music was initially created on the slave plantations in America and was forbidden in communist Poland. It was played in secret up until 1954, and in the 1960s, jazz festivals rekindled the flame and it's now inextinguishable. If you don't care for jazz music, you should give it another chance in Krakow. You'll hear a mellow, almost classical version of it at *Piano Rouge*. At *U Muniaka* and *Alchemia*, they play a more experimental and modern version that's free-spirited, avant-garde and punk-like. At *Club Prozak 2.0*, the jazz is easy to dance to. Finally, you'll hear spontaneous jam sessions in pubs like *Piec Art*.

MOUNDS OF MYSTERY

Is it really true that the *Wanda Mound (Kopiec Wandy)* in Nowa Huta and the ● *Krakus Mound (Kopiec Krakusa)* in Podgórze are part of an astronomical calendar? Well, it's true that on certain Celtic and Slavic holidays, if you're standing on one of the two mounds, the sun sets and rises directly above the other one. Some claim the Krakus Mound (16-m/52-ft-high) is the tomb of Krakow's legendary founder, while the other one belongs to his daughter. Even archaeologists say the mounds' elevations date back to pre-Christian times and were artificially raised. Located around Krakow, there are two more man-made mounds – the *Piłsudski's Mound* made in 1937 and the *Kościuszko's Mound* from 1820. Both are named after Poland's greatest national heroes. The latter is especially worth visiting; from the mound's summit, you'll have a particularly beautiful view of Krakow.

THE POPE'S CREAM PIE

If you need a coffee break while exploring the city, order a piece of *kremówka papieska* while you're at it. This delicious cream pie is named after Pope John Paul II (born in Wadowice) and nicknamed the 'papal *kremówka*'. According to legend, Karol Wojtyła (John Paul II's birth name) is said to have eaten 18 slices of these calorie bombs during a friendly bet. After graduating from high school, Wojtyła moved to Krakow and lived on the Vistula River until he was elected Pope in 1978. During this time, he studied philology at Jagiellonian University where he wrote poetry and plays, which are still being performed in Polish theatres today. During WWII and the Nazi Occupation of Poland, he studied theology at a forbidden 'underground seminary' and was forced to work in a chemical factory and quarry. From the Ulica Franciszkańska, you can see the 'papal window' of the Bishop's Palace. It's always decorated with burning candles and white-yellow flowers in memory of Wojtyła's speeches. In 1946, he was ordained a priest and later became an archbishop in 1963. Together with the Independent Self-governing Labour Union 'Solidarity', Wojtyła stood against the socialist rulers of Poland. Although John Paul II died in 2005 and was canonised in 2014, you'll find memorials of him all throughout the city, giving the impression that his legacy still lives on today.

THIS RIVER HAS IT ALL!

The Vistula River is one of Krakow's biggest tourist attractions. Although it's forbidden to go swimming in the river, it's still a popular place for water sports and boat excursions (see p. 105) to e.g. the Benedictine Abbey in Tyniec. During the summer months, the Vistula becomes a great place to go partying. The locals really enjoy being near the river, so much so that they dock their boats and spend the entire day just eating, drinking and dancing. If you're intending to visit overnight, you're welcome to stay in one of the hotels floating on the water. You'll find that most of the boat moorings are at the bottom of Wawel Hill and in Kazimierz on Bulwar Czerwieński.

On the other bank of Bulwar Wołyński, you'll find a sandy beach and a floating swimming pool. Many festivals are held along the Vistula, and it's a popular place for families to go picnicking. If you want to go on a walk or for a jog, the loveliest area is the section between Wawel Hill and the bridge in Podgórze (*Most Piłsudskiego*). A new pedestrian bridge (*Kładka Ojca Bernatka*), which is illuminated at night, connects Kazimierz with Podgórze.

Bust of Pope John Paul II: Memories of a defiant Krakow hero

SIGHTSEEING

CITY WHERE TO START?
The square **Rynek Główny (114 B–C3)** *(🕮 D4–5)* is the best place to start your sightseeing tour as it is the most central. Many of the main attractions and the best restaurants are found in this area. The square is for the most part pedestrianised, but you can park your car either on a side street *(parking zone tickets at machines: 3 Pln for the first hour, then 3.50 and 4.10 Pln; weekends free),* at the car park near the Franciscan Church *(Plac Wszystkich Świętych 5)* or at Westerplatte 18. All tram lines will take you into the centre of town.

Krakow's historic centre is small, charming and easy to explore on foot. From here, you can take a one-horse carriage ride back to the times of the Austrian Habsburg Monarchy.

The centre initially seems to be dominated by the city's past. The Wawel complex towers over the Old Town and boasts a royal castle and a magnificent cathedral. Church towers dot Krakow's skyline, and impressive sights are visible both on and off the Royal Route. The scenery changes, however, as you begin to walk through Planty, a park encircling the Old Town. Here, you'll discover where the city's medieval walls once stood and find plenty of magnificent areas and pathways to relax in. The Vistula also offers many leisure activities. You can take a

The city of churches. Krakow is the best place to experience Poland's history and its centuries-long, multifaceted tradition

river cruise, rent a paddle boat or enjoy a meal at one of the riverboat restaurants. On the Rynek Główny main square, life remains lively, vibrant and Mediterranean-like. Around Planty Park, you'll find Krakow's many districts (e.g. Kazimierz, Zwierzyniec and Kleparz) which are usually easy to walk to from the Old Town. You'll only need a tram or bus to visit one of the outer suburbs (e.g. the workers' district Nowa Huta). Founded by the Russian occupiers, Nowa Huta was initially planned to be the ideal socialist city.

NORTHERN OLD TOWN

There's always a lot going on in this part of Krakow! You'll stroll past high-end restaurants and the city's most exorbitant shops and boutiques.

Be happy you're visiting Krakow today and not a few centuries ago! Even if you were sent here on an official mission, you still had restrictions. At that time,

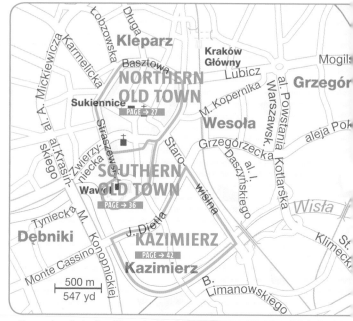

The map shows the location of the most exciting districts. On the pages indicated, you'll find a detailed map of that district and all the sights located there which are indicated by number.

it was impossible to stroll through Krakow's beautiful Gothic city centre. Even if you were well known or had a high rank, visitors were never allowed to veer from the Royal Route, which, unfortunately, never passed by the most significant and exciting buildings. Today, the route starts at St Florian's Gate, goes down Ulica Floriańska and leads into the city centre. It crosses Rynek Główny and goes uphill to the Wawel complex, which boasts a castle and cathedral. Still undamaged by all the wars, Krakow's most beautiful churches, palaces and buildings stand today to tell of the city's history. They were built between the 13th and 15th centuries during the city's golden age when Krakow was considered the country's largest city.

■ KOŚCIÓŁ ŚW. WOJCIECHA (CHURCH OF ST ADALBERT)
(113 E5) (*D5*)

Possibly Krakow's smallest and oldest church from the 11th century. Its greatest treasure is hidden below in the crypt. Next to it is an exhibition on the Market Square's history where you can see how the level of the plaza rose more than 2.50 m/8.2 ft over the centuries. With 80 available seats, beautiful chamber concerts take place here regularly *(tickets on site)*. *Museum: Mon–Sat 10am–4pm | admission 5 Pln | Rynek Główny 2*

■ FORTIFICATIONS
(114 C1–2) (*E3–4*)

Invaders must have had a really hard time trying to take over Krakow in the Middle

Ages. To start, the city was surrounded by a strengthened double wall 3 m/10 ft thick. If that wasn't enough, 47 fortified towers and a deep moat around the city also protected Krakow from intruders. The guilds had the responsibility of protecting the bastions, the place where they also stored part of their arsenal. To top it off, the *Krakow Barbican*, a round, fortified complex with seven slender turrets, was added in the 15th century. These measures kept the city safe for 400 years. However, as was the case for most major European cities, these medieval fortifications were demolished once protective walls and towers were deemed useless. What remains today is just a small section of the inner wall, two of its bastions, the arsenal, the Barbican and the main entrance gate. The Barbican and the walls are open to the public. Once you reach ☽ the top, you'll have an interesting view over the city. A permanent exhibition shows the development and history of the complex, and further details are provided in two or three temporary shows every year. In summer, you'll find artists offering their pictures for sale inside the walls outside, and INSIDER TIP regular concerts and jousting festivals also take place here.

Leave the fortification complex through the main gate, the *Porta Gloriae*, to return to the city; this is where the Royal Route begins, and it opens up a spectacular view of the Ulica Floriańska with St Mary's Church and the Rynek Główny. *April–Oct daily 10.30am–6pm | admission 8 Pln (Barbican and walls) | entrance to the walls from Ulica Pijarska*

MARCO POLO HIGHLIGHTS

★ **Collegium Maius**
Copernicus was here! Krakow's oldest university building → p. 30

★ **Kościół Franciszkanów (Franciscan Church)**
An art nouveau gem → p. 30

★ **Kościół Mariacki (St Mary's Church)**
Wealth, splendour and the famous altar by Veit Stoss → p. 31

★ **Czartoryski Museum**
They are still renovating, but that's no excuse to miss the ancient art on display here! → p. 33

★ **Rynek Główny (Market Square)**
Krakow's magic makes itself felt on this spacious square → p. 33

★ **Sukiennice (Cloth Hall and Picture Gallery)**
The magnificent hall on the Market Square → p. 34

★ **Ulica Kanonicza (Kanonicza Street)**
Destination Middle Ages: stroll, explore, admire → p. 40

★ **Zamek Królewski (Royal Castle)**
Renaissance gem full of treasures → p. 41

★ **Kościół Bożego Ciała (Corpus Christi Church)**
Monumental Gothic splendour → p. 42

★ **Synagoga Remuh (Remuh Synagogue)**
Impressive purity full of Jewish culture → p. 44

★ **Fabryka Schindlera (Schindler Factory)**
Thought-provoking exhibition on the Nazi occupation → p. 46

★ **Auschwitz-Birkenau**
Never forget! Essential confrontation with the horror of the Nazis → p. 50

3 COLLEGIUM MAIUS ★ ●
(114 A3) *(ᗯ C5)*

Founded by King Kasimir the Great in 1364, Jagiellonian University is Poland's oldest academic institution, and the Collegium Maius is the city's oldest university building. In the arcades around the Gothic inner courtyard, you'll find

Gothic splendour in St Mary's Church

crystalline vaulting which is especially worth seeing. The structure looks more like a monastery than a university. If you miss the popular carillon, which happens every two hours and ends with the song 'Gaudeamus Igitur' ('So Let Us Rejoice'), find a seat at a café in the original Gothic cellar and take a trip back to the 15th century, the time in which Nicolaus Copernicus studied here. Up until the 1960s, the astronomer's monument stood in the courtyard. Along with Pope John Paul II, he is one of the university's most famous students.

You also have to visit the University Museum! There's a 30-minute tour *(call to book an English tour: 126 63 13 19)* that takes you through the magnificent Gothic rooms of the library, the professors' dining room and the main lecture hall. *Polish tours every 20 minutes (see website for booking): April–Oct. Mon, Wed 10am–2.20pm, Tue, Thu 10am–5.20pm, Fri 10am–1.30pm, English tours: Mon–Fri 1pm, Nov–Mar Mon–Thu 10am–2.20pm, Fr 10am–2.30pm, no tour: Sat 10am– 1.30pm; carillon (free admission) 9am, 11am, 1pm, 3pm, 5pm | Admission from 12 Pln, free on Sat | Ulica Jagiellońska 15 | www.maius.uj.edu.pl*

4 KOŚCIÓŁ FRANCISZKANÓW (FRANCISCAN CHURCH) ★
(114 B4) *(ᗯ D5–6)*

The best time to visit this neo-Gothic church is on sunny days. Large parts of its interior date back to the period when art nouveau was popular. Unfortunately, these parts are pretty dark, making it difficult to see the art. Therefore, **INSIDER TIP** choose a sunny day for your visit – you'll be able to see the art nouveau works by Stanisław Wyspiański under a much better light. He painted the walls with flowers and stars and created the glass windows for the presby-

tery as well as the one above the main entrance with the 'Creation of the World'. *Daily 6.30am–8pm but not during the fair | Plac Wszystkich Świętych 5*

5 KOŚCIÓŁ MARIACKI (ST MARY'S CHURCH) ★ (114 C3) *(ᴍ E5)*

St Mary's Church's greatest treasure is its 14th-century *Krakow Altarpiece* cre-

ated by Veit Stoss. This artist came from Nuremberg, Germany, devoting twelve years of his life to this masterpiece. He started in 1477. Made of oak and lime wood, it's 11×13 m/36×42 ft in size and painted and decorated with gold leaf. The altar is gradually being renovated and should be restored to its original medieval design by 2023. You used to be able to only see the art once a day for a short period of time. However, now it's always open despite the renovation. In the south wing, you'll find a statue of the crucified Christ. Built by Veit Stoss, it's made out of one piece of sandstone. In case you didn't know, St Mary's Church has been modified and expanded several times. This explains the variety of architectural styles seen both in and outside the church.

sion to church 10 Pln | Plac Mariacki 5 | mariacki.com

6 INSIDER TIP **KOŚCIÓŁ ŚW. ANNY (CHURCH OF ST ANNE) (114 A3) (ω C4)**

A place for academics! Since the early 18th century, students and professors of the nearby university have been coming to this elaborately decorated three-nave

Green lung and open-air gallery: the Planty around the Old Town

You'll have the most beautiful view of the city from the church's 82-m/269-ft *tower (April–Oct 9.10am–11.30am and 1.10pm–5.40pm | admission 15 Pln).* But remember that INSIDER TIP *tickets are limited,* so it's best to get your ticket the day before or as soon as the church's ticket window opens (see times below). Every hour on the hour, you'll hear the song *Hejnał,* 'Poland's second national anthem', being played from the higher of the two towers. *Mon–Sat 11.30am–6pm, Sun 2pm–6pm | admis-*

basilica. Artist Balthasar Fontana decorated the church with stucco and illusionistic paintings. Each work attempts to create a sensation of three-dimensionality and depth. Designed by court architect Tylman van Gameren, the church was completed in 1703. Not only is it Krakow's best example of late baroque architecture, but it's also one of Poland's finest 18th-century buildings. It also has a beautiful *carillon (Mon–Sat 6.58am, 9am, noon, 3pm, 6pm, 9pm | Sun is the same with the exception 7am and 11.48am).* The church organ is also a feast for the eyes and ears. *Only during Mass | Ulica św. Anny 11 | kolegiata-anna.pl*

7 MUZEUM CZARTORYSKICH (CZARTORYSKI MUSEUM) ★
(114 C2) (*𝄞 E4*)

As far as we know, the country's oldest museum was still being renovated at the time we published this travel guide, so do double check online. If possible, make sure to visit the Czartoryski family's art collection. Despite the renovation, the *Gallery of Antiquities* is still open *(Tue– Sun 10am–4pm | admission 8 Pln | Ulica Pijarska 8)*. *Ulica św. Jana 19*

8 MUZEUM FARMACJI (PHARMACY MUSEUM) (114 C2) (*𝄞 E4*)

If you've ever wondered how dragon blood is used in medicine, you'll find the answer here. This museum's design is that of an old pharmacy. From the cellar up to the attic, you'll find remedies both bizarre and pharmaceutically useful and gain some interesting insight into the history of medicine since the Middle Ages. Marvel at old scales, exotic animals, ostrich eggs, amulets, poisons, medical musk products and minerals. Dried bats hang from the ceiling, and there's a room full of herbs in the attic. Brochures are also available in English. *Tue 12pm– 6.30pm, Wed–Sat 10am–2.30pm | admission 9 Pln | Ulica Floriańska 25 | www. muzeumfarmacji.pl*

9 PLANTY
(114–115 A–D 1–5) (*𝄞 C–F 3–6*)

Turning swords to ploughshares and fortress walls and secluded parks. The 4-km/2.5-mi-long green belt that encircles the Old Town was placed where the medieval city walls and moats used to be. Take in the fresh air while strolling through the Planty, a park filled with paths, ponds, flower beds and meadows. It's a great way to experience the city's outdoors and from another angle. An added attraction is the ● largest collection of outdoor monuments from the 19th and 20th centuries. The park's sculptures are by great Polish artists, like the painter Artur Grottger. Other sculptures show fictional characters taken from Polish literature. You'll also find numerous benches with QR codes. Scan them with your smartphone to learn about the works of writers and poets, such as Stanisław Lem, Jerzy Pilch, Joseph Conrad, Georg Trakl and Herta Müller (see p. 24). The 50-acre green area is perfect **INSIDER TIP** for joggers.

10 RYNEK GŁÓWNY (MARKET SQUARE) ★ ●
(114 B–C3) (*𝄞 D4–5*)

'Windows? No thank you!' It's hard to believe, but this is how the wealthiest citizens thought back when they had their residences and palaces around the

LOW BUDGET

● Most of the museums' permanent exhibitions are free on Sundays or Mondays. Contact the museums for more information.

Free ● classical concerts are held frequently in many of the churches. For dates and times, look for posters around the city *(TIP: 'wstęp wolny' means free admission)*.

☮ The most environmentally friendly and inexpensive way to travel is on bike. You can rent and return bikes all over Krakow *(more info on p. 101)*.

Market Square. You may also be surprised by the buildings' narrow facades. They were built this way so the rich could avoid paying higher taxes. Back then, tax prices were determined depending on how many windows the homeowner had in their home. This is why you'll sometimes see buildings with no more than two windows – just enough to let the light in! A fairly odd rule for the largest medieval square in Europe (200 × 200 m/656 × 656 ft)!

Krakow's fascinating Market Square never sleeps and has always represented the city's cultural centre. In the summertime, it's a place that almost feels like Italy – not only because of all the pigeons but also for the Renaissance architecture seen at Cloth Hall and in the residential buildings. The Sukiennice (Cloth Hall) and St Mary's Church are among the great market's highlights. Until the 19th century, the square was strewn with grocery stores, big and small buildings, and the town hall. This was, however, all demolished after 1820. Today, the townhouses on the square show an array of architectural styles – from Gothic to 20th-century design. All year round, the square puts on festivals, concerts and exhibitions. Seasonal markets are held around Christmas and Easter.

11 SUKIENNICE (CLOTH HALL AND ART MUSEUM) ★
(114 B3) (*Ω D5*)

Cloth Hall, located in the middle of Market Square, is one of Krakow's many famous landmarks. It used to be the place where the city's most sought-after goods were traded, including salt and all kinds of fabric. Krakow used to be on the old salt-trading route and enjoyed special privileges, making it the wealthiest city in the Polish kingdom. The structure was initially erected in the 14th century and then alter-

ed in the 16th and 19th centuries. The long hall has external arcades and an original Renaissance parapet adorned with grotesque faces. The Cloth Hall still flourishes as a centre of commerce. At the souvenir shops on the ground floor, you can buy amber jewellery, leather goods, wood carvings and other arts and crafts.

On the first floor, you'll find the *Galeria Sztuki Polskiej XIX wieku (The Sukiennice Museum with 19th-Century Polish Art) (Tue–Sat 10am–6pm, Sun 10am–4pm | admission 16 Pln, audio guide 7 Pln, combined ticket for all branches of the National Museum (permanent exhibitions) 50 Pln (see p. 47) | Rynek Główny 1–3)*. It boasts a wide collection of large historical paintings, Polish portraits and landscapes. The museum's ☼ INSIDER TIP *Café Szał (daily 10am–11pm | admission to the terrace without a museum ticket, 2 Pln)* with a view of St Mary's Church is a joy for the senses.

Take a walk through medieval Krakow and beneath the market square to find

Stylish trading centre with fabulous view: from the Cloth Hall across the Market Square

the ● *Rynek Podziemny (Underground Market Square Museum) (April–Oct Mon 10am–8pm, Tue 10am–4pm, Wed–Sun 10am–10pm, Nov–March Mon, Wed–Sun 10am–8pm, Tue 10am–4pm, closed 2nd Mon in month | admission 21 Pln, audio guide 5 Pln, Tue free admission (book early!) | Rynek Główny 1 | www.podziemia rynku.com)*. The cemetery and miniature versions of small shops that used to be on the Market Square are especially fascinating. You will also be able to see objects unearthed during excavations under the square. TV screens show the most important aspects of Krakow's history (also in English).

▣ TEATR IM. J. SŁOWACKIEGO (JULIUSZ SŁOWACKI THEATRE) (114 D2) (*m E4*)

First Vienna, Paris and then Krakow – having first opened in 1893, this is the city's most beautiful theatre. It boasts a variety of styles and motifs seen in neo-baroque architecture, similar to the theatres built under the Habsburg Monarchy. It's like a miniature version of the Paris Opéra Garnier. Although the performances are only in Polish, you really shouldn't miss seeing the interior's extravagant splendour. The INSIDERTIP original main curtain is one of the theatre's many highlights as it's raised off the ground rather than rolled up. The allegorical scene shown on the front displays the personification of artistic inspiration, comedy and tragedy. *Plac Świętego Ducha 1 | www.slowacki.krakow.pl*

▣ WIEŻA RATUSZOWA (TOWN HALL TOWER) ● ⤴ (114 B3) (*m D5*)

To punish offenders, rather than throwing them into an underground torture chamber, they could have just chased them up and down the steep steps of this 14th-century, 70 m/230 ft-high tower. Although the climb to the top isn't easy, it's still worth the trip. From the tower's ⤴ top floor, you'll have a INSIDERTIP splendid view over the city. In result of the town hall being torn down in 1820, this structure is now the only one standing on the square's western side. The climb to the top will also take you back in time as a branch of the Historical Museum is found here. On the ground floor, you'll find a 15th-century parlour, which was used as a treasury during the Middle Ages. Here on the first floor is where the councillors used to hold meetings. The cellar, which was where the prison and aforementioned torture chamber used to be, now houses a café and small theatre. *April–Oct daily 10.30am–6pm | admission 9 Pln | Rynek Główny 1*

SOUTHERN OLD TOWN

A fire-breathing dragon and a castle full of treasure! Draping over the city, the silhouettes of the Wawel Cathedral and the Royal Castle already promise plenty of exciting and impressive stories for history fans to discover.

Before you make your way up the hill you should take a closer look at the bishops' palaces on Ulica Kanonicza. Although remnants of Pope John Paul II are seen all over Krakow, they are especially more present here. Karol Wojtyła lived on Ulica Kanonicza while he was bishop and arch- bishop and worked in the Wawel Cathedral on the hill.

▮▮ KATEDRA ŚW. STANISŁAWA I ŚW. WACŁAWA (ŚWIDNICA CATHEDRAL) ● ⬆⬇ (114 B6) (𝄄 D7)

Are those really the bones of the Wawel Dragon hanging up left of the entrance? Or are they those of a whale, mammoth and rhino? Either way, they serve an important purpose: on the day they fall to the ground, we'll know the world is coming to an end. Unfortunately, we still don't have enough evidence to prove this is true. Nonetheless, the Cathedral of St Stanislaus and St Wenceslaus, as the Krakow Cathedral is officially known, stands on Wawel Hill, close to the castle, and is hands down the most important church in all of Poland on account of its symbolic meaning and function. The place in which Poland's kings used to be crowned is the third church on this site. Construction began in the 14th century and it was altered countless times over the centuries; it now combines all architectural styles from Gothic to modern. Serving as a burial site for Poland's regents, the cathedral houses a large number of royal coffins. President Lech Kaczyński and his wife, who both perished in a plane crash in April 2010, were also laid to rest in the crypt.

FIT IN THE CITY

If you're craving a good workout, the best jogging and cycling routes are around *Błonia* **(112 A6)** *(𝄄 A5)*. The paved runways on the edge of the Old Town run along the Rudawa River at times and encompass a massive field 118 acres in size. The most beautiful *cyc- ling tour* takes you along the Vistula River from Krakow towards the Benedictine Abbey of Tyniec. No worries if you can't be bothered cycling back. Just jump on one of the ferries docked along the Wawel in Krakow. For information on *bike rentals* see p. 101.

Where Poland's kings were crowned and buried: Wawel Cathedral

The three-nave basilica is flanked by two Gothic chapels – the one on the right, seen from the entrance, the *Holy Cross Chapel*, is especially noteworthy. It was decorated with Russian-Byzantine frescoes in the 15th century and is also the site of the marble grave Veit Stoss created for the Polish King Kazimierz Jegiellończyk. A baroque silver sarcophagus with the relics of St Stanisław occupies the central place in the cathedral.

The cathedral itself is rather small for a royal and episcopal church, so there are a high number of chapels surrounding it. Two are particularly precious: the *Kaplica Zygmuntowska (Sigismund Chapel)* and the *Kaplica Wazów (Waza Chapel)*. The first is described as the 'pearl of the Renaissance north of the Alps'. The purity of its style and perfect symmetry is still appreciated today and not only by art lovers. It was created out of red Hungarian marble, combined with white stone, by the Italian master Bartolommeo Berrecci in the 16th century.

The Waza Chapel represents the epitome of baroque art and thought and is completely decorated with black marble. The cathedral decorated its front door with skeleton bones to remind visitors of the transience of life.

While you're here, you should definitely visit the ☀ *Wieża Zygmuntowska (Sigismund Tower)* with its fabulous panoramic view. The bell at the top shares the tower's name and is the largest one in Poland. It weighs 12 tons and boasts a diameter of 2.5 m/8.2 ft! According to legend, all those who touch the bell are guaranteed eternal love and happiness for the rest of their days.

On display in *The Cathedral Museum* are objects associated with Pope John Paul II, which were taken from the treasury. These include chalices, monstrances and garments. *April–Sept Mon–Sat 9am–5pm, Sun 12.30pm–5pm, Oct–March at the cathedral: Mon–Sat 9am–4pm, Sun 12.30pm–4pm, museum closed Sun; photography is prohibited | ● free admission* to nave and part of the southern side nave; royal tombs, Sigismund Tower, various chapels and museum 12 Pln, audio guide 7 Pln | Wawel 3 | www.katedrawawelska.pl/en

🔲 KOŚCIÓŁ ŚW. ANDRZEJA (ST ANDREW'S CHURCH) (114 B–C5) (𝓂 D–E6)

Don't let the church's austere exterior put you off. Despite its Romanesque style and unique double towers, it's one of the city's oldest churches. Dating back to the 11th century, this fortified church is equipped with embrasures and up to 1.60 m/5.2 ft-thick walls. Often used to protect the Krakow people, it was even utilised in 1241 when the Tartars ran riot through the town. The interior of this small, three-nave church is even more beautiful. It boasts an altar made of black marble and a ship-shaped pulpit. The mere sight of this baroque golden structure is enough to leave you in awe. *Daily 7am–6pm | Ulica Grodzka 54*

🔳 KOŚCIÓŁ ŚW. PIOTRA I PAWŁA (SAINTS PETER AND PAUL CHURCH) (114 B–C5) (𝓂 D6)

This church enables visitors to see the earth's rotation up close. You can witness this phenomenon on certain days when the church lowers a Foucault pendulum from the ceiling. The pendulum's swing proves the earth rotates. This aisleless church built of red bricks and light-coloured granite is Poland's first baroque church. Construction started in 1597 and lasted until 1619 due to static problems with the church's dome. The house of worship is an exact copy of the Jesuit Church of the Gesù in Rome – some people go so far as to say that the proportions in Krakow are even better than those of the church it was modelled on. The church often puts on summer concerts; check the posters at the entrance for exact information. The building is also cold in summer, so don't forget your pullover if you attend a show. *Daily 6.30am–7pm, except during services | Ulica Grodzka 52a | apostolowie.pl*

The twelve Apostles welcome the faithful to the Church of Saints Peter and Paul

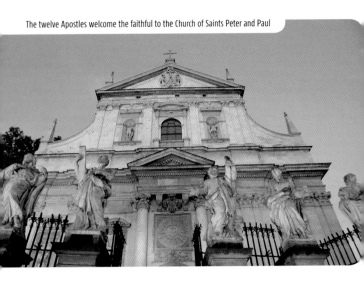

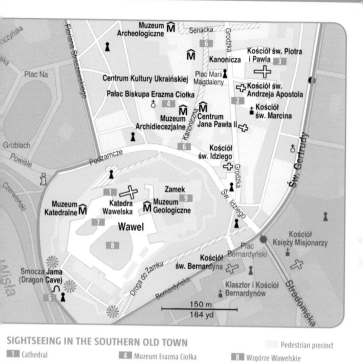

SIGHTSEEING IN THE SOUTHERN OLD TOWN

- **1** Cathedral
- **2** Kościół św. Andrzeja
  (St Andrew's Church)
- **3** Kościół św. Piotra i Pawła
  (Saints Peter and Paul Church)
- **4** Muzeum Erazma Ciołka
- **5** Smocza Jama (Dragon's Cave)
- **6** Ulica Kanonicza
- **7** Wawel Zaginiony
  (Lost Wawel)
- **8** Wzgórze Wawelskie
  (Wawel Hill)
- **9** Zamek Królewski
  (Royal Castle)

░░░ Pedestrian precinct

4 MUZEUM ERAZMA CIOŁKA (THE ERAZM CIOŁEK PALACE) (114 B5) *(ØJ D6)*

This museum is one of the National Museum's many branches. Inside, the palace exhibits priceless 14th to 16th-century paintings and sculptures in its *Art of Old Poland* collection. These include a large number of Gothic altarpieces. **INSIDERTIP** The hall, which is devoted to baroque Polish funeral customs, is particularly impressive. Religious music plays in the background and various coffins and pictures of coffins are on display, a unique form seen in the Polish art scene.

You'll also come across *Orthodox Art of the Old Republic*, which shows icons and objects used in the liturgy of the Eastern Church. These Orthodox paintings are part of one of the oldest and most valuable collections in Central Europe. Below the beautifully restored cellar, you'll find a collection of sculptures and decorative elements taken from important architectural sites in Poland. The music comes from a stone instrument called a lithophone. *Tue–Fri 9am–4pm, Sat 10am–6pm, Sun 10am–4pm | admission 9 Pln, Audio guide 7 Pln, Sun free entry | Ulica Kanonicza 17 | www.mnk.pl*

SOUTHERN OLD TOWN

▨ 5 SMOCZA JAMA (DRAGON'S CAVE) (114 A6) (*Ш C7*)

Luckily, the story of the virgin-eating dragon who lived in a cave ends with his sweet demise. Although a mere legend, perhaps the dragon part is true as archaeologists

castle. This makes it well worth your time to take a INSIDER TIP ▶ walk on a warm evening past the illuminated buildings. The street is named after the people who lived on it. The canons of the cathedral chapter were the bishops' advisers

Ulica Kanonicza: Grand palaces of former clergymen line the street

found bones of prehistoric animals here. The dragon's cave is entered at the top of the Wawel Hill and exited at the Vistula. The path is illuminated in such a way that the mythical figure could be around any corner. And then – bam! – there he is – standing at the exit in the form of a fire-breathing metal sculpture! *May/June daily 10am–6pm, Jul/Aug 10am–7pm, Sept/Oct 10am–5pm | Admission 3 Pln | Wawel 5 | www.wawel.krakow.pl*

▨ 6 ULICA KANONICZA (KANONICZA STREET) ★ (114 B5) (*Ш D6*)

Each of the buildings on this narrow road is worth observing. A lot goes on here during the day with it being the last section of the Royal Route leading to the

and built their palaces here at the foot of the hill. The facades and richly decorated portals of the houses at numbers 1, 3, 9, 13 and 15 are especially interesting. Behind their Gothic facades, you'll often find Renaissance arcaded courtyards reminiscent of the Royal Castle.

▨ 7 WAWEL ZAGINIONY (THE LOST WAWEL) (114 B6) (*Ш D7*)

What did the Wawel look like from the 10th to 14th centuries? Travel back in time with the help of models, films and an INSIDER TIP ▶ almost completely preserved early-Romanesque rotunda from the 10th/11th century. NOTE: Tickets are limited! *April–Oct Mon 9.30am–1pm, Tue–Fri 9.30am–5pm, Sat/Sun 10am–*

5pm, Nov–March Tue–Sat 9.30am–4pm, Sun 10am–4pm | admission April–Oct 10 Pln, otherwise 8 Pln, April–Oct Mon, Nov–March Sun free admission | Wawel 5 | www.wawel.krakow.pl

8 ■ WZGÓRZE WAWELSKIE (WAWEL HILL) 🌿 (114 A–B 5–6) (𝄞 D7)

Wawel Hill offers one of the best views of the city – a sight most likely enjoyed by the people living here during the Palaeolithic Age. This assumption results from the fact that archaeologists found proof of people settling here long before the areas around Krakow were Christianised in the 10th century. The fact that the hill not only had fresh springwater but was also surrounded by the Vistula on all sides made it a strategically ideal location. Today, it is no longer possible to see where the Vistula originally flowed because the river was diverted in the 19th century.

9 ■ ZAMEK KRÓLEWSKI (ROYAL CASTLE) ★ (114 B6) (𝄞 D7)

Since its first 11th-century construction, the Royal Castle in Warsaw has caught fire so many times that you'd think matches would be off limits by now. It was, after all, a fire that led King Zygmunt Stary to work as an architect. He was the first in his country to have the residence reconstructed in Renaissance style (1504–1536). Italian artists from Florence created the monumental three-storey building with its arcaded inner courtyard. It was the official residence of Poland's monarchs until the end of the 16th century – that is until the building caught fire again. In response, King Zygmunt III Waza and his court moved to Warsaw. This time, the castle was reconstructed in baroque style but only served as their weekend residence. Over the years, many others occupied, plundered and finally renovated it.

Today, there's a museum in the castle, and each room is open to the public. Among the other treasures is a collection of 16th-century tapestries said to be some of the most beautiful in the world. King Zygmunt August commissioned them to be made and woven in Brussels using cotton, gold and silver thread, and silk. They were made to measure for the rooms and originally covered most of the walls; they recount three of the most important stories from the Bible: Adam and Eve, the Tower of Babel, and Noah's Ark. *Reprezentacyjne komnaty królewskie (State Rooms): April–Oct Tue–Fri 9.30am–5pm, Sat/Sun 11am–5pm, Nov–March Tue–Fri 9.30am–4pm, Sat/Sun 10am–4pm | admission April–Oct 20 Pln, Mon 9.30am–1pm free, Nov–March 16 Pln, Sun 10am–4pm free; ticket still required for free admission. Prywatne komnaty królewskie (Royal Private Apartments): as above, closed on Sun | admission 24 Pln, sign up for guided tours in English at the information centre (see below)*

The crown jewels are on the ground floor of the oldest section of the castle. Here, you'll see the Gothic remains of its earlier structure and, more importantly, the *Szczerbiec* – the coronation sword of the Polish kings. Weapons from the 15th to 19th centuries, as well as medieval armour, are on display in the nearby armoury. *Skarbiec Koronny i Zbrojownia (Crown Treasury and Armoury) (April–Oct Mon 9.30am–1pm, Tue–Fri 9.30am–5pm, Sat/Sun 11am–6pm, Nov–March Tue–Sat 9.30am–4pm | admission April–Oct 18 Pln, Nov–March 16 Pln)*

You can buy tickets to these exhibitions either at the entrance gate *(Brama Herbowa | end of April–end of Oct, Mon 9am–11.45am, Tue–Fri 9am–3.45pm, Sat/Sun 9.30am–3.45pm)* or at the *Information Centre (Centrum Promocji i Informacji)*. Expect long queues during the high season. Tickets are limited and only valid during a certain time. You can avoid the queues by coming early. You'll also find toilets, souvenir shops, a sub-post office, restaurants and cafés at the information centre. NOTE: Photography is prohibited inside the castle. Rucksacks must be left at the cloakroom, and visitors are not permitted to carry sharp objects (pocket knives, nail files, etc.). In summer, you'll have a lovely view from the ☼ terrace at INSIDER TIP *Café Słodki Wawel. April– June Mon–Fri 9am–4.45pm, Sat/Sun 10am–4.45pm, July/Aug Mon–Fri 9am– 5.45pm, Sat/Sun 9.45am–5.45pm, Sept/ Oct Mon–Fri 9am–4.45pm, Sat, Sun 9.30am–4.45pm, Nov–March Tue–Sat 9.15am–2.45pm, Sun 9.30am–2.45pm | Wawel 5 | www.wawel.krakow.pl*

KAZIMIERZ

Cafés, pubs, clubs and artists: Kazimierz is popular for its bohemian charm, but don't forget about its (often tragic) Jewish history.

This trendy district is walking distance from the centre and a popular hang-out area for partygoers and night owls. At Plac Nowy (the heart of the district), you'll find plenty of cafés, pubs and clubs that stay open late in summer. Kazimierz is especially enjoyable in the evening with its klezmer concerts and Jewish restaurants on Ulica Szeroka.

What's now a beloved district was once an independent city up until the 19th century. It had a marketplace, town hall and many magnificent monasteries. Rich in Jewish history, the Jews who resettled here from Krakow in the 15th century had their homes in an enclosed section around Ulica Szeroka. It boasted seven synagogues, cemeteries, businesses and schools. Everything was peaceful until

1941 when the National Socialist occupiers deported the Jews to the ghetto in the Podgórze district of Krakow.

Life changed after that, and Kazimierz came to a standstill – that is, until Steven Spielberg came to shoot his film 'Schindler's List' here. The tourists soon followed and everything was in full swing. The Jewish history was present again, but with it came the memories of suffering. *You can either walk to Kazimierz (15 min from Wawel Hill via Ulica Stradom and Ulica Krakowska; from Poczta Główna via Ulica Starowiślna) or by tram 3, 6, 8, 13 (Wawel to Plac Wolnica) and 24 (Poczta Główna to Miodowa).*

■ KOŚCIÓŁ BOŻEGO CIAŁA (CORPUS CHRISTI CHURCH) ★
(118 B4) (𝄞 F8)

The parish church in Kazimierz on the former marketplace is one of the city's most beautiful Gothic churches. Legend has it that when the church was built, people saw a strange light for weeks above the construction site. The workers digging here also discovered a monstrance that had disappeared from a church in Krakow. Particularly worth seeing in this monumental, medieval church are its main altar and boat-shaped pulpit. *Daily 6am–8pm, except during services | Ulica Bożego Ciała 26*

■ KOŚCIÓŁ PAULINÓW NA SKAŁCE (PAULINE CHURCH 'ON THE ROCK') (117 E5) (𝄞 D9)

Legend has it that St Stanisław, the country's most important patron saint, was beheaded where this 18th-century baroque church now stands and his body was then thrown into the nearby well. People claim its water took on healing powers, making the well a place of pilgrimage. A procession in honour of St Stanisław is organised every year in May – it

Jewish tradition also lives on in the restaurants of Kazimierz

begins at the cathedral and ends at the three-nave basilica with its magnificent, black marble portal. *Daily 6am–8pm, except during service | Ulica Skałeczna 15*

◼ **INSIDER TIP** MUZEUM GALICJA (GALICIA JEWISH MUSEUM)
(118 C3) (*∅ G8*)

This private museum is devoted to paying tribute to the Holocaust victims. The exhibition 'Traces of Memory' depicts the history of Jewish life in Galicia and is exceptionally well documented. The photos on display here were taken by photographer Chris Schwarz. His pictures take visitors on a journey through the eastern regions of modern-day Poland and Ukraine. Inside, you'll also find a café and well-stocked bookstore which offers plenty of literature on Galicia and Jewish history. Visit their website for more information. *Daily 10am–6pm | admission 16 Pln | Ulica Dajwór 18 | www.galiciajewishmuseum.org*

◼ PLAC NOWY (NEW SQUARE)
(118 B3) (*∅ F8*)

There are plenty of restaurants, hip clubs and landmark pubs to visit here. At *Alchemia* (see p. 72), guests are served outdoors in the summer. People flood the district's square, making it a popular place among the youth. What makes this square special, however, is how it still retains is historical function. Even today, although the goods sold here have changed, the square's still a place for trade. The Okrąglak hall, for example, was a kosher poultry abattoir until 1939. Today, they sell delicious **INSIDER TIP** *zapiekanka* at small snack bars. This cult snack costs around 10 Pln and is a kind of Polish pizza. The most popular stand is the *U Endziora*, but you'll have to queue before ordering.

A food and flower market is held on the Plac Nowy daily, as is **INSIDER TIP** a flea market at the weekend. Here, you'll find clothing, bags and jewellery for sale (including designer articles at excellent

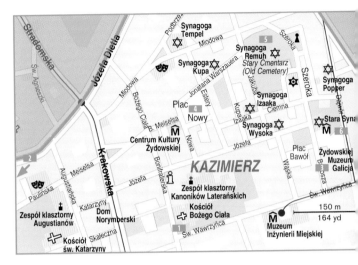

prices). On Saturdays, antiques like old Jewish silver can be purchased.

5 SYNAGOGA REMUH (REMUH SYNAGOGUE) ★
(118 C3) (*∅ F7*)

The seven synagogues in Kazimierz have all been preserved, and regular services are still held in the renovated 16th-century Remuh Synagogue on the Sabbath (after sunset on Friday and on Saturday) and other Jewish holidays. The interior is very simple and tastefully decorated, in keeping with the commandment in the Old Testament of not using decorations from the living world in art. The orthodox division into separate sections for men and women is still discernible in the synagogue's architecture.

The neighbouring *Old Jewish Cemetery (Stary Cmentarz)* is no longer in use but is well worth visiting to see its many old gravestones. The largest tomb is that of Moses Isserles Remuh, a rabbi of the community in the 16th century. Today, Jews from all over the world still make pilgrimages to his grave as they believe that any prayers said there will be heard. You will see remnants of *macevas* (Jewish gravestones) that have been found during renovation work in the 1950s on the eastern wall to the right of the entrance to the cemetery. The locals call it the 'Wailing Wall' after the counterpart in Jerusalem. Men have to cover their head if they want to visit the synagogue or cemetery – if you do not have a cap with you, you can borrow a *kippah* free of charge in the synagogue. *Mon–Thu 9am–4pm (to 6pm in summer), Fri 9am–3.30pm (to 5.30pm in summer) | admission 10 Pln | Ulica Szeroka 40*

6 SYNAGOGA STARA (OLD SYNAGOGUE) (118 C3) (🕮 F8)

Converted into a museum during the Renaissance, this old Gothic synagogue now houses a Jewish cultural museum. The temple dates from the end of the 15th century and is the oldest synagogue in Poland. You will notice the traditional separation into different sections for men and women even before you enter. The museum tells the story of everyday Jewish life: knives used for slaughtering animals in accordance with Jewish laws, circumcision instruments, crowns and bells for the Torah. *April–Oct Mon 10am–2pm, Tue–Sun 9am–5pm, Nov–March Mon 10am–2pm, Tue–Thurs, Sat/Sun 9am–4pm, Fri 10am–5pm | admission 10 Pln, free on Mon | Ulica Szeroka 24*

IN OTHER DISTRICTS

CRICOTEKA (118 C5) (🕮 G9)

If you're looking at an old power station below a massive steel structure, you've made it to the Centre of Documentation of the Art of Tadeusz Kantor (1915–1990). Together with his experimental theatre group Cricot 2, this theatre director, painter, performance artist, set designer, writer and actor achieved European acclaim for his play 'Dead Class', a work that broke down conventional boundaries between the visual arts and theatre. The structure also offers a bookshop, a café and an unparalleled view of

The 600-year-old Synagoga Stara: Impressive and beautiful in its simplicity

the city from the top floor. *Tue–Sun 11am– 7pm | Ulica Nadwiślańska 2–4 | admission 10 Pln, Tue free | www.news.cricoteka.pl*

EUROPEUM (112 C5) (*B5*)

A further branch of the National Museum, this time located in a 17th-century warehouse which has been renovated in exemplary fashion. Some 100 paintings and sculptures stand for seven centuries of European art. Pleasant INSIDERTIP museum café *(only open in summer)*. *Tue–Sat 10am–6pm, Sun 10am–4pm | admission 9 Pln | Plac Sikorskiego 6*

FABRYKA SCHINDLERA (SCHINDLER FACTORY) ★ ● (119 F5) (*J9*)

The Museum of the City of Krakow established the permanent exhibition on the fate of its Jewish and non-Jewish citizens 'Krakow under Nazi Occupation 1939– 1945' on the premises of Oskar Schindler's Deutsche Emailwarenfabrik (German Enamelware Factory) (DEF). On the three floors of the museum, visitors can get a taste of what life was like for the people living in Krakow. You'll learn about the horrible conditions in the ghetto and the long-awaited liberation by the Red Army in January 1945. The office has been preserved in its original state in memory of Oskar Schindler who produced enamelware and later ammunition for the German Army in his factory. Although Schindler was originally only interested in making money, he decided to save more than 1100 Jews after the Nazis liquidated the ghetto in March 1943; he pretended they were needed to produce materials essential to the war effort. Schindler's action became world-famous with Steven Spielberg's film 'Schindler's List' in 1993. The tour *Memory Trail (Trasa Pamięci) (www.mhk.pl/memory-trail)* is part of a combined ticket for admission to the *Eagle Pharmacy (see p. 49)* and *Ulica Po-*

morska (see p. 50), the Gestapo prison, costing 32 Pln. *April–Oct Mon 10am–4pm, Tue–Sun 9am–8pm, 1st Mon/Month till 2pm, Nov–March Mon 10am–2pm, Tue– Sun 10am–6pm | admission 24 Pln, free on Mon (come early!), book tickets online if possible, recommended for children 14 and up | Ulica Lipowa 4 | www.mhk.pl*

DOM MEHOFFERA (JÓZEF MEHOFFER HOUSE) (112 C4) (*B4*)

At this museum, surrounded by original furnishings, family photos and souvenirs, you'll feel as if you're in the home of one of Poland's greatest art nouveau painters: Józef Mehoffer (1869–1946). In 1932, Mehoffer bought the house where Stanisław Wyspiański was born, a neoclassicist villa in Nowy Świat. This is where he and his family lived until his death. On display are his paintings and projects, such as the glass windows he designed for the Freiburg Cathedral. The INSIDERTIP garden next to the house, where Mehoffer created many of his pictures, is an oasis of greenery right in the middle of the city and perfect for a break from sightseeing. *Tue–Sat 10am–6pm, Sun 10am–4pm, garden and museum café Ważka 10am–9.30pm | admission 9 Pln, Sun permanent exhibition free | Ulica Krupnicza 26 | muzeum.krakow.pl*

MOCAK MUZEUM SZTUKI WSPÓŁCZESNEJ W KRAKOWIE (MUSEUM OF CONTEMPORARY ART) (119 F5) (*J9*)

At the Museum of Contemporary Art (MOCAK), you'll find the latest trends in modern art, both in Poland and worldwide. They offer a permanent exhibition and interesting temporary shows. Parts of the Schindler Factory were used to construct the museum. *Tue–Sun 11am– 7pm | admission 14 Pln | ● free on Tue | Ulica Lipowa 4 | www.mocak.com.pl*

MUZEUM NARODOWE (NATIONAL MUSEUM) (112 B5) (*M A5*)

Everyone knows Leonardo da Vinci's 'Mona Lisa', but what about his ● 'Lady with an Ermine'? The young lady's name is Cecilia Gallerani, and she was once the lover of Duke Lodovico Sforza of Milan. Those who have seen her say she's even

collection of Polish arts and crafts and the '*Gallery of 20th-century Polish Art*', which is particularly good. The museum also houses a new shop and the beautiful café *Tribeca Coffee. Tue–Fri 9am–5pm, Sat 10am–6pm, Sun 10am–4pm | admission 10 Pln, permanent exhibition free on Sun | Aleja 3 Maja 1 | www.mnk.pl*

The Museum of Contemporary Art: A thrilling contrast to Krakow's pervasive history

more enchanting than the famous Mona Lisa in Paris. Her painting has been hanging in the museum's main building since the Polish state acquired it and will remain here until at least the end of 2019. Founded in 1879, the museum's holdings grew so quickly that it became necessary to move some of its departments to other locations. They include the *Picture Gallery in Cloth Hall*, the *Czartoryski*, *Erazma Ciołka* and *Europeum* museums, and the *Józef Mehoffer House*. You can buy a INSIDER TIP combined ticket for 50 Pln which entitles you to entry into all branches of the National Museum. The most interesting sections in the main building are the military exhibition, a

MUZEUM WITRAZU (STAINED GLASS MUSEUM) (112 B6) (*M B5*)

If you liked the stained glass windows in the Wawel Castle and Franciscan Church, you'll be interested to know they were made in the Zelenski family's workshop, the namesake of this museum. Not only can you see the art on display here, but you can also watch the windows being made. Take a ● two to three-hour course and make your own glass object. A stylish café and small souvenir shop are also inside. *Tue–Sat 12pm–5pm, English tours every hour, reservations not required | admission 35 Pln, courses start at 180 Pln | Aleja Krasinskiego 23 | tel. 5 12 93 79 79 | muzeumwitrazu.pl*

IN OTHER DISTRICTS

NOWA HUTA (U E–F 2–3) (*M 0*)

Visiting Nowa Huta is like entering another world and is an exciting and rewarding trip. It's a long drive, so plan at least half a day for your visit. This district of Krakow was built from the grounds up in 1949 under Russian occupation. The Russians wanted to build a model communist city boasting a complete infrastructure, wide streets and many parks. Its inhabitants, who were transported en masse from the rural parts of Poland, were given flats of modern design in concrete blocks to live in. The government also gave them a job at the Vladimir Lenin Steelworks, which was conveniently located next door. The experiment ultimately failed after long-established residents rejected the idea behind Nowa Huta, which was also meant to act as a counterweight to Krakow's bourgeois intellectual culture. Those residents who grew up in the countryside refused to work within a socialist framework. Instead, they wished to continue their conventional life, farming livestock (sometimes from the comfort of their own balcony!) and attending church regularly.

Churchgoers put Nowa Huta on the map with its *Ark of the Lord Church (daily 6.30am–6pm, except during services | Ulica Obrońców Krzyża 1 | bus 139 Arka)*, the first church in this socialist model community. The people living in Nowa Huta fought for more than ten years to get permission to build the church and many paid with their lives in the conflicts that took place. After an additional ten years of construction, it was finally consecrated by the then archbishop Karol Wojtyła in 1977.

Its modern architecture reminds one of Le Corbusier's famous chapel in Ronchamp. The building in Nowa Huta is shaped like a large boat with the cross as its mast. It was mainly constructed of round, light-coloured stones that the faithful had collected from rivers. The most impressive features of the interior are the wooden roof construction and enormous bronze sculpture of the crucified Christ. The tabernacle contains a crystal that the crew of 'Apollo 11' brought back from the moon.

Until today, it has not been possible to merge Nowa Huta and the 250,000 people living there with the other districts of Krakow – the differences in culture and social structure are simply too great. In addition, the workers' district is now struggling with unemployment. After the steelworks were privatised, many of the workers were made redundant.

The most interesting architecture in Nowa Huta comes from the 1950s and 1960s and can be seen on *Plac Centralny (Central Square)*, the starting point for the four main roads and a pedestrian avenue *(Aleja Róż)*. The neoclassicist buildings onsist of large and sunny apartments, and there are spacious parks nearby. The architecture from the later phase (1970s and 1980s) is completely different. Built quickly and cheaply, high, grey blocks of flats – with a planned 86 ft² per person – set the tone in this section of town. Nowa Huta is fairly spread out; you should plan at least half a day for your visit. *Tram 1 Teatr Ludowy, 4 Plac Centralny, 15 Cystesów, bus 139 Arka*

OGRÓD BOTANICZNY (BOTANICAL GARDENS) ● (U C3) (*M H–J 4–5*)

The most beautiful seasons in the Botanical Gardens are INSIDER TIP summer and early autumn when the lilies, peonies and irises are in full bloom. The former observatory now houses the *Botanical Garden Museum*, including the largest collection of orchids in Poland. The

The huge Jesus sculpture at the Ark of the Lord Church is an impressive sight

oldest tree in the gardens is a 500-year-old oak. The easiest way to get to this green oasis is on foot from the Market Place via Ulica Kopernika. *April–Oct daily 9am–5pm, greenhouses Sat–Thu 10am–4pm | admission 9 Pln | Ulica Kopernika 27*

PODGÓRZE (121 E4) (*☉ E–J 9–10*)

In March 1941, Nazis came to today's Podgórze to set up a Jewish ghetto within a 49-acre section of the suburb. Some 16,000 people were forced to live where only 3000 had lived previously – in unbelievably cramped conditions. Today, there is no wall or any special plaque to show where the ghetto was. Instead, an installation of metal chairs on *Plac Bohaterów Getta (Ghetto Heroes Square)* recalls its destruction in March 1943 when all of the furniture and personal belongings of the people living there were simply thrown out of their windows. The inhabitants were then either shot in the ghetto or transported to concentration camps. Close by is the *Apteka Pod Orłem (Eagle Pharmacy) (Mon 10am–2pm, Tue–Sun 9am–5pm, closed on the 2nd Tue/Month | admission 10 Pln, free on Mon | Plac Bohaterów Getta 18 | mhk.pl),* the only one to supply medicine to the Jews living in the ghetto. Many of them, mostly children, were saved by the pharmacist Tadeusz Pankiewicz, who hid them from the Nazi thugs in the cupboards in his shop. Today, the pharmacy houses a museum. The highly informative, interactive exhibition has been re-vamped in recent years and is well worth a visit. It relates the history of the ghetto and the people who tried to survive there, focusing on the pharmacy as a place of refuge and on Pankiewicz and his staff who gave them refuge.

ULICA POMORSKA (HISTORICAL MUSEUM) (112 B1) (*☉ B2*)

During WWII, this building was once the headquarters of the Gestapo, the official secret police. Now a museum, its exhibition not only marks the history of the Nazis' reign of terror but also of the Great Purge during the Soviet era. In the former Gestapo cells, you'll find more than 600 words, prayers and pleas that were once etched into the walls by prisoners. The sight is quite moving. *April–Oct Tue–Sun 10am–5.30pm, Nov–Mar Tue/Wed, Fri 9am–4pm, Thu 12pm–7pm, Sat/Sun 10am–5pm | admission 9 Pln, prison cells are free to enter | Ulica Pomorska 2 | www.mhk.pl/branches/pomorska-street*

FURTHER AFIELD

AUSCHWITZ-BIRKENAU ★
(0 0) (𝄞 0)

No other name brings back more memories of the unimaginably horrible deeds perpetrated by the Nazis than that of the Auschwitz-Birkenau concentration camp. More than 1.2 million people – mostly Jews – were murdered in the largest German extermination camp. Today, there is a memorial site and museum on the 470-acre site near Oświęcim (about 45 km/28 mi from Krakow). The organisation of what was originally a labour camp shows just how the occupiers went about their work with such perfidious technocratic coldness: the prisoners in Camp III (Monowitz) had to labour in the factories of the Buna Werke (IG Farben), while those in Auschwitz I were forced to build roads and houses. The largest section of the camp was where the living barracks, prison, death cells, administration and the home of the camp's commander Rudolf Höss and his family were located. You can still see the cynical sign 'Arbeit macht frei' (Work sets you free) above the main gate to Auschwitz I.

The real horror took place in Auschwitz II (Birkenau): people were murdered in four large gas chambers and then incinerated in the crematoriums – the wooden housing barracks were only temporary. A visit to Auschwitz is a highly emotional – and shocking – experience; make sure that you, and especially your children, are well prepared for what you will encounter. Plan about 5 hours for your visit. There's a free shuttle bus between both camps. Due to the high demand for tickets, it's best to book online (at least one month in advance!). You could also book an organised tour from Krakow *(approx. 150 Pln)* with *Cracow City Tours (see p. 105). Daily Dec 7.30am–2pm, Jan, Nov 7.30am–3pm, Feb 7.30am–4pm, March, Oct 7.30am–5pm, April, May, Sept 7.30am–6pm, June–Aug 7.30am–7pm, (You may stay up to 90 minutes after close); Auschwitz Camp I: April–Oct 10am–4pm guided tours only (4 hrs), before 10am and after 4pm also without tour; Auschwitz Camp II: enter*

with or without tour | book an English tour at visit.auschwitz.org; only small bags allowed | admission 50 Pln, free without tour | Więźniów Oświęcimia 20 | Oświęcim | auschwitz.org/en | Getting there: minibuses from Krakow railway station or by car via Dw 780, Dk 44 or A4 towards Oświęcim, follow the signs for 'Muzeum Auschwitz'

KOPALNIA SOLI WIELICZKA (WIELICZKA SALT MINES) (121 E5) (*ⓜ 0*)

The salt mines in Wieliczka (10 km/6 mi to the south) are one of the main attractions in the environs of Krakow and have been a Unesco World Heritage Site since 1978. From the 13th century on, the mines were one of the most important sources of revenue for Krakow and the entire kingdom; in its heyday in the 15th century, the salt trade accounted for more than 30% of the town's total income. Mining continued until well into the 20th century but now very little salt is extracted. There are more than 30 km/186 mi of labyrinthine paths on nine underground levels. The main attraction on the 'Tourist Route' – in addition to the 20-m/66-ft-high chambers and a salt lake – is the Kaplica św. Kingi (Chapel of the Blessed Kinga) where everything down to the chandelier is made of pure salt. The graduation tower *(admission 9 Pln, combination ticket 6 Pln)* offers a great view from its ☆ observation platform. Underground, the temperature is only 14 degrees Celsius, so INSIDER TIP don't forget your pullover! Buy your tickets online or in advance in *Ulica Wiślna (same opening times as the mine)* in Krakow. *April–Oct daily 7.30am–7.30pm, Nov–March 8am–5pm | English tours 10.45am, 2.15pm, 4.10pm | admission (only with tour) starts at 89 Pln | Ulica Daniłowicza 10 | Wieliczka | www.salzbergwerkwieliczka.de | Getting there: bus 304 (Filharmonia to Wieliczka kościół, bilet aglomeracyjny, 4 Pln) or by car via A4 towards Tarnów as far as Wieliczka exit, follow signs for Kopalnia (mine)*

Salt, salt and more salt: The Wieliczka Salt Mine in the Chapel of St Klinga

FOOD & DRINK

Although Krakow offers great Polish cooking, the international cuisine served is also superb. In short, the food here is anything but bland!

In Krakow, Polish cuisine is usually inexpensive, but delicious all the same. Even during socialist times, Krakow had a great culinary reputation. Many of the city's Gothic cellars have been renovated into romantic restaurants. It's a dining experience like no other where brick walls and round arches give the interior its rustic feel. In summer, the restaurants and cafés bring their tables outside, placing them along lively streets or into romantic courtyards. Want to try Polish beer? Two great brews are *Żywiec* and *Okocim*.

Today, fine Polish cooking is marked by fish (i.e. trout, carp) and game. Krakow's traditional food includes *pierogi* (filled dumplings) and *gołąbki* (cabbage rolls). Crayfish soup, venison and duck are also classic dishes. Soups like *barszcz* (made of beetroot), *żurek* (flour soup) and *zupa borowikowa* (boletus mushroom soup) are also popular Polish dishes and are served in almost all restaurants. It's still true that Poles eat a lot of meat, but pork, veal, poultry and lamb (sometimes served with traditional groats) are no longer the only options. Vegetarian Polish food and even veganism are growing popular in Krakow's culinary scene. Even *pierogi*, the national dish, is also made meatless now and has been popular for quite some time.

Krakow's history has had a massive influence on the city's international culinary scene. The Jews introduced kosher

Photo: Duck served the Krakow way – with a side of groats and mushrooms

Polish or international cuisine? Pizza or *pierogi*? Whatever you choose, Krakow has a well-deserved reputation for culinary variety

and sweet-and-sour dishes. During the Habsburg period, immigrants made Czech, Hungarian and Austrian food popular and they brought their sacred coffee culture with them. Over time, Spanish, Asian, Mexican, Greek and Indian food also began to be served in Krakow. And let's not forget the Italian cooking! Krakow also has many specialities, like *obwarzanek*. This ring-shaped bread is braided, baked to perfection and usually sold on the streets. The Polish twist on pizza is called *zapiekanka*. This tasty snack is a toasted, open-faced sandwich topped with mushrooms, vegetables or ham. Most restaurants, including the best and most expensive ones, are in the city centre and Kazimierz. Lunch is served around midday and is Krakow's most important meal of the day. Dinner is usually served between 6pm and 7pm, and almost all restaurants open daily and close late unless otherwise noted. Many bistros start serving breakfast at 8am and most cafés sell snacks, too. Smoking is prohibited in all restaurants.

Ever tried the world's most expensive coffee? At Pożegnanie z Afryką you can

CAFÉS & CAKE SHOPS

JAMA MICHALIKA (114 C2) (*M E4*)

Serving delicious snacks and cake, this café is one of the city's oldest. The interior still boasts the same art nouveau from 1895. At the start of the 20th century, many students from the art academy came here to sell their paintings, proving art can be a profitable profession after all. *Daily | Ulica Floriańska 45 | tel. 124 22 15 61 | www.jamamichalika.pl*

KAWIARNIA NOWOROLSKI ☆ (114 B3) (*M D5*)

A traditional, chic Viennese-style café serving amazing cake. Made with three different kinds of chocolate, the cake is to die for! Grab a table on Market Square and enjoy a view of St Mary's Church. *Daily from 7.30am | Rynek Główny 1/3 | tel. 124 22 47 71 | www.noworolski.com.pl*

CAFÉ MANGGHA ☆ (117 D4) (*M C8*)

Located in the Japanese Museum with a superb view of Wawel Hill from the terrace. A wide variety of teas **INSIDER TIP** served in traditional Japanese clay pots and small cups. Japanese beer and sour-cherry tart. *Closed Mon | Ulica Marii Konopnickiej 26 | tel. 608 67 93 08 | cafe manggha.com.pl*

POŻEGNANIE Z AFRYKĄ (114 C3) (*M E4*)

I've died and gone to coffee heaven! The coffee varieties are endless. Order a fresh cup of joe or take a bag home with you. The world's most exclusive and expensive coffee is also sold here: Kopi Luwak from Indonesia. Only 300–400 kg (660–880 lbs) are produced each year. Check out their small **INSIDER TIP** museum with coffee-making utensils of yesteryear. *Daily | Ulica św. Tomasza 21 | tel. 124 21 23 39 | www.pozegnanie.com*

SŁODKI WENTZL (114 B3) (*M D5*)

Ice cream to go? No problem! But if you want to do it right, grab a table outside and order something sweet. You'll have a beautiful view of Cloth Hall. Delicious cakes, tarts and desserts are offered.

Rynek Główny 19 | tel. 124 29 57 12 | slodkiwentzl.pl

ICE CREAM PARLOURS

LODY SI GELA 🟢 (118 C6) (*∅ F10*)

Ever tried 'beer ice cream'? 'Gorgonzola ice cream with nuts'? Well, it's all home-made, vegan, gluten-free and organic! You have to give this ice cream a try! More of their creative flavours include lavender and rose petal. *Daily 11am–8pm, in summer until 11pm | Ulica Staromostowa 1 | tel. 6 09 47 55 37 | sigela.pl*

INSIDER TIP PRACOWNIA CUKIERNICZA STANISŁAW SARGA (118 C3) (*∅ G8*)

This mini shop only offers six kinds of ice cream – but maybe that's exactly why it's the best in town. Chocolate ice cream with great chunks of chocolate and strawberry ice cream with whole strawberries – fantastic! You might have to queue a while though to be served. *Closed Sun | Ulica Starowiślna 83 | tram 13 św. Wawrzyńca*

SNACK BARS

CHIMERA ★ (114 B3) (*∅ D5*)

Do you prefer fresh vegetables over meat? Then you've come to the right place! The salad bar is 30 m/98 ft long and placed outside under a glass roof. Order what you'd like and pay either 14 Pln for a small salad or 19 Pln for a large one. Grilled meat, game and soup dishes are also served. The restaurant boasts a heated fireplace in winter and a 14th-century cellar for dining. *Świętej Anny 3 | tel. 122 92 12 12 | www.chimera.com.pl*

KROWARZYWA 🟢 (114 B2) (*∅ D4*)

No life had to be spared to give the patties at this burger joint their delicious taste! Vegan burgers, wraps, hot dogs and sandwich kebabs, all bursting with fresh vegetables. Homemade lemonade and smoothies are also available! *Closed Mon | Ulica Sławkowska 8 | tel. 5 51 77 71 36 | krowarzywa.pl/en*

INSIDER TIP PIEROŻKI U VINCENTA (120 C3) (*∅ c3*)

A restaurant serving over 30 different kinds of *pierogi* dumplings. There's one called *kreplach*, which is a Jewish speciality. They also have *pelmeni*, which is a Russian delicacy stuffed with meat. *Daily | Ulica Juliusza Lea 114 | tel. 126 36 66 23 | bus 704 Jadwigi z Łobzowa*

INSIDER TIP PIZZATOPIA (114 A2) (*∅ C4*)

Create your pizza masterpiece! Choose your favourite toppings and get creative. Everything is placed on light and fluffy dough and takes less than three minutes to bake. They also have delicious salads, homemade lemonade and

---

MARCO POLO HIGHLIGHTS

★ **Chimera**
Huge selection of fresh salads – in the charming inner courtyard or in front of the fire → p. 55

★ **Wesele**
Polish cooking with international flair→ p. 57

★ **Orzo**
Healthy food served in a green, jungle-like atmosphere → p. 58

★ **Wentzl**
Absolute luxury and unique game dishes in one of the best restaurants in Krakow → p. 57

LOCAL SPECIALITIES

barszcz – a beetroot soup served with eggs, potatoes and croquettes. Also a typical Christmas meal with small dumplings stuffed with sauerkraut
bigos – meat, sausage, sauerkraut and mushroom stew. The luxury version is served with red wine
gołąbki – cabbage leaves stuffed with a filling of rice and meat; a vegetarian version with rice and mushrooms is also common. Served in tomato or mushroom sauce (photo left)
obwarzanek – similar to a bagel, this ring-shaped bread is braided together and baked to perfection
pierogi – large dumplings made with a variety of fillings, prepared both with and without meat. *Pierogi ruskie* is made with boiled potatoes and curd cheese while *Pierogi z mięsem* contains meat. *Pierogi z kapustą i grzybami* is filled with sauerkraut and mushrooms. You can also find them stuffed with strawberries *(z truskawkami)* or plums *(z śliwkami)* when the season is right
rosół – meat bouillon with noodles, usually served to families on Sunday
sernik – cheesecake
żurek – sour flour soup with boiled egg, sausage, garlic and potatoes (photo right)

bottled craft beer, all served on wooden platters! *Ulica Szewska 22 | tel. 12 570 06 51 95 | www.pizzatopia.com*

TRZY PAPRYCZKI (114 B4) (*ᗝ D6*)
Take a trip to Italy in this rustically decorated restaurant serving more than 20 different kinds of pizza. Also antipasti, grilled meat, pasta and salads. *Daily | Ulica Poselska 17 | tel. 12 292 55 32 | www.trzypapryczki.krakow.pl*

FARINA (114 C2) (*ᗝ E4*)
Fish? In Krakow?! Well, of course! This is INSIDER TIP the best fish and seafood restaurant in town. They offer seasonal dishes and everything from oysters to gilthead (excellent meat and pasta dishes are also available). *Daily | Ulica św. Marka 16 | tel. 12 422 16 80 | www.farina.com.pl*

HAWEŁKA – RESTAURACJA TETMAJEROWSKA (114 B3) (𝄐 D5)

This restaurant has served exclusive Polish and international cuisine in an original fin-de-siècle ambience since 1876. The staircase is adorned with paintings by Polish art nouveau artists. There is a wide choice of game dishes and fish, and a slightly less expensive version of the restaurant on the ground floor. The *Hawełka Cake Shop* in the entrance passage offers sweet things to take away. *Daily mid-March–mid-Nov from 11am, at other times noon–10.30pm | Rynek Główny 34 | tel. 12 42 20 6 31 | www. hawelka.pl*

STUDIO QULINARNE (118 B4) (𝄐 F9)

It's hard to tell now, but this stylish restaurant was once used to service buses. Now they serve creative five, seven and nine-course gourmet meals instead. The tastes are exceptional and everything is made from local ingredients. There is a small outdoor dining area and a cocktail bar. *Daily from noon | Ulica Gazowa 4 | tel. 12 4 30 69 14 | www.studioqulinarne.pl*

SZARA ☒ (114 B3) (𝄐 D5)

Restaurant in a medieval townhouse with Gothic arches and art nouveau frescoes. Exquisite international cooking: *raraka* (potato fritters with caviar), reindeer or salmon tartare. INSIDER TIP A less expensive lunch is served between noon and 3pm, which you can eat outside in summer while enjoying the view of St Mary's Church. The bar has excellent cocktails. *Daily 11am–11pm | Rynek Główny 6 | tel. 12 4 21 66 69 | www.szara.pl*

WENTZL ★ ● ☒ (114 B3) (𝄐 D5)

With this restaurant being over 200 years old, you can't help but wonder who used to eat here. Established in 1792, this is one of the best restaurants in the city. Call in advance to reserve a table with a great view overlooking the Market Square. If you like game or classic European cuisine, you'll feel right at home as well as ennobled by its historical atmosphere. They also have a large wine selection. *Rynek Główny 19 | tel. 12 429 52 99 | restauracjawentzl.com.pl*

WESELE ★ ☒ (114 C4) (𝄐 D5)

Boasting a view of the Market Square, this restaurant, located on two floors, serves modern Polish cooking and Krakow specialities. Try delicious combination platters like Polish potato pancakes with sour cream or duck with honey-dipped pears. *Daily noon–11pm | Rynek Główny 10 | tel. 12 4 22 74 60 | www.weselerestauracja.pl*

WIERZYNEK ☒ (114 B3) (𝄐 D5)

Over 650 years ago, the monarchs of Europe had a feast here lasting 20 days and nights. Today, it's the city's most famous restaurant. Your feast won't last as long,

LOW BUDGET

On Wednesday, restaurants often offer a daily lunch special *(danie dnia)*, which is a lot less expensive than the dishes on the evening menu. *From 15 Pln*

'Milk Bar Cafeterias' (Bar Mleczny) are popular among students and serve inexpensive soups, salads and meat dishes. We recommend *Bar pod Temidą (Ulica Grodzka 43)*

Keep your stomach (and your wallet) full! You'll find many *kebab stands* on Ulica Floriańska and Ulica Grodzka with vegetarian options. *From 10 Pln*

of course, but you'll be treated to a royal experience nonetheless. Overlooking the Market Square, the rooms are all beautifully decorated. Delicious Polish and international specialities are served. Evening meals are by reservation only. *Rynek Główny 15 | tel. 124 24 96 00 | wierzynek. pl/en/*

RESTAURANTS: MODERATE

CHŁOPSKIE JADŁO (114 B4) (*𝄞 D5*)
Take a short break from the diet and indulge! This restaurant, boasting an old farmhouse interior, serves country-style Polish cuisine. It's admittedly rich and fatty, but boy is it delicious! To start, try the sour cucumbers on lard bread and follow it with some plum and garlic pork chops. *Ulica Grodzka 9 | tel. 7 25 10 05 32 | www.chlopskiejadlo.pl*

DINE IN THE DARK (114 B4) (*𝄞 D5*)
'Dining in the dark' is also popular in Krakow, but the experience here has a twist. We don't want to spoil it, but it involves Polish cuisine (vegetarian option available). Book early online. *At the restaurant Piwnicapod Kominkiem: Ulica Bracka 13 | tel. 124 30 21 30 | www.dineinthedark.pl*

KLEZMER HOIS ● (118 C2) (*𝄞 F8*)
Jewish food. Kosher but without rabbinical supervision. Authentic atmosphere with embroidered tablecloths. Old, dark furniture and paintings commonly seen in middle-class homes of the 20th century. An unforgettable dining experience that takes you into another world, especially when attending one of the klezmer concerts (usually at the weekend). *Ulica Szeroka 6 | tel. 124 111 2 45 | www.klezmer.pl | tram 24 Ulica Miodowa*

FAVOURITE EATERIES

Meals in a Farmhouse
Camelot Café (114 C2) (𝄞 D4)
Great salads, famous apple pie and homemade spirits – all served in a farmhouse parlour. The interior features simple wooden cupboards, glass cabinets and hand-painted boxes. The walls exhibit a naïve art collection by Polish painter Nikifor, and the outdoor dining area is also lovely. *(Ulica św. Tomasza 17 | tel. 124 21 01 23)*

Welcome to the Jungle!
Orzo ★ ◎ (114 C2) (𝄞 D4)
The food made here follows the motto 'people – music – nature'. The menu offers burgers, pizza, salad and the rice-shaped pasta called 'Orzo'. Healthy ingredients are added, and the tastes

blend wonderfully together with the restaurant's jungle-like atmosphere. Escape the city smog and breathe in the clear air created by the hanging plants, small shrubs and trees. *(Lipowa 4a | tel. 122 57 10 42 | www.orzo.pl)*

France, Sweet France... *Zakładka Food & Wine (118 C6) (𝄞 F10)*
Oh là là! An original French bistro with excellent cuisine and a varied menu. In addition to French dishes, they serve local products including goats cheese and freshly caught trout from Ojców National Park. Open seven days a week, but ensure you make a reservation if it's the weekend! *(Mon from 5pm, Tue–Sun from 12pm | Ulica Józefińska 2 | tel. 124 42 74 42 | zakladkabistro.pl)*

At home down on the (Polish) farm: great atmosphere at Chłopskie Jadło

POD ANIOŁAMI (114 B4) *(📖 D6)*

The finest Polish cuisine served in a Gothic cellar. Grilled meat, pies (hare pie with cranberries), and duck with apples and served with dark wholemeal bread, red cabbage and sour pickles. In summer, guests are served in a small courtyard outside in the garden. Good wine list and Polish mead. *Ulica Grodzka 35 | tel. 12 430 21 13 | www.podaniolami.pl*

RESTAURACJA TRADYCJA

(114 B3–4) *(📖 D5)*

Does Polish folk dancing increase one's appetite? There's only one way to find out! Every Saturday at 7pm, guests are invited to a folklore dining and dancing experience (Participation is optional). If you'd like something unique, try the Polish-Italian main course. The restaurant is on Market Square in a Renaissance building where Hieronim Pinocci lived in the 16th century. He was the Italian king's secretary and published Poland's first newspaper. *Rynek Główny 15 | tel. 12 424 96 16 | tradycyja.pl*

RESTAURANTS: BUDGET

DOBRA KASZA NASZA (114 B3) *(📖 D5)*

Groats anyone?! These ground cereal grains are made of buckwheat, millet or pearl barley and are part of Polish cuisine. This restaurant serves them with salad on a wooden plate and covers them with a meat-based or vegetable-based sauce. *Rynek Główny 28 | tel. 5 31 62 64 47 | www.dobrakaszanasza.pl*

KOLANKO NUMER 6 (118 B3) *(📖 F8)*

This place offers a great breakfast buffet, international cuisine and all kinds of sweet and savoury crêpes. Guests are served on the beautiful green terrace in summer *Ulica Józefa 17 | tel. 5 09 66 99 59 | www.kolanko.net | tram 8 Plac Wolnica*

POLAKOWSKI (118 B2) *(📖 F7)*

There are many of these self-service restaurants serving homemade Polish dishes, soups and meat. Try the one at *Ulica Miodowa 39* or *Plac Wszystkich Świętych 10 | polakowski.com.pl*

SHOPPING

WHERE TO START?

CITY WHERE TO START?
In addition to the **Galeria Krakowska** and **Galeria Kazimierz**, the most popular places to go shopping are on **Ulica Floriańska** and **Ulica Grodzka**. This is where you will find fashion, shoe stores and jewellery shops, not to mention a number of art galleries and antique dealers. There are also many souvenir shops in and around **Rynek Główny**, the Market Square and **Cloth Hall**. If you're looking for original styles, you'll find plenty of unique jewellery and out-of-the-ordinary souvenirs on **Ulica Józefa** in Kazimierz (take tram 6 or 8 to Plac Wolnica).

While shopping in Krakow, not only will you find all the popular brands and chains commonly found in other major cities, but you'll also come across many shops and items unique to this one. You'll enjoy shopping around the city centre surrounded by its historical buildings.

Most shops line the Market Square, the Royal Route, Ulica Floriańska and Ulica Grodzka. Here, you'll find everything from delicatessen shops to fashion boutiques, art and bric-a-brac, where you can buy a wide variety of souvenirs. In Kazimierz, you'll find charming modern art galleries, designer jewellery shops and a popular Sunday flea market. Shopping in Krakow, however, has become limited since Poland introduced its new Sunday trading law in 2018. Today, Sunday shopping is

The flair of a time-honoured trading centre continues to make rummaging and shopping a very special experience in Krakow

only possible for a short time and, come 2020, you won't be able to go Sunday shopping at all *(general opening hours see: Travel Tips)*. If you're in the market to buy a unique souvenir, visit one of the city's amber jewellery shops (see p. 64). Poland is also known for selling high-quality spirits, including *Żubrówka (bison grass vodka), Krupnik (honey liqueur)* and *Żołądkowa Gorzka (herbal vodka)*. If you need something for the kids, they'll love getting a Wawel Dragon or one of the traditional wooden toys for sale.

BOOKSTORES

DE REVOLUTIONIBUS ●
(114 B4) (*ሠ D5*)

Reading 'De revolutionibus orbium co-elestium' may improve your Latin, but at *De Revolutionibus Books&Cafe*, you can have your cake, coffee and smoothie, too! You'll find plenty of Polish and English books, including Copernicus's literary masterpiece 'On the Revolutions of the Celestial Spheres'. *Ulica Kanonicza 11 | www.derevolutionibus.com.pl*

You will find modern Polish art for your living room in the Gołogórski Gallery

EMPIK (114 B3) (*Ⅲ D5*)

This Krakow music and bookstore has been in operation since 1610, making it the first bookstore ever founded in Europe. The interior has been completely renovated, exhibiting old portals, impressive ceilings and a beautiful cafè. *Rynek Główny 23*

DELICATESSEN

KREDENS KRAKOWSKI (114 C2) (*Ⅲ E4*)

With six locations around the city, this delicatessen offers speciality sausage, marmalade, honey, tea, coffee and sweets. All items are traditionally packaged, and their products make for a great souvenir. *Ulica Florianska 42 | krakowskikredens.pl*

SHOPPING CENTRES

GALERIA KAZIMIERZ ●
(119 D–E3) (*Ⅲ H7*)

This is Krakow's most impressive shopping centre. The building has an original design and a bricked exterior. Inside, you'll find over 100 shops, cafés, restaurants and even a cinema. *Mon–Sat 10am–9pm | Ulica Podgórska 34 | www.galeria kazimierz.pl | take tram 3, 9, 19, 24 to św. Wawrzynca, then a 5-minute walk along the Vistula*

GALERIA KRAKOWSKA (115 D1) (*Ⅲ F3*)

A shopping centre with over 270 shops covering a floor space of 390,000ft². You'll find brand-name sports, fashion and cosmetic articles for sale, as well as cafés and restaurants. *Mon–Sat 9am–9pm | Ulica Pawia 5 | www.galeria krakowska.pl*

PASAŻ HANDLOWY 13 (114 B3) (*Ⅲ D5*)

What do the words 'Gothic', 'Renaissance', 'metal' and 'glass' have in common? Well, they all describe this exclusive department store on Market Square. Just seeing it is worth the trip! In addition to many Polish fashion stores, you'll also find **INSIDER TIP** exclusive delicacies from around the world. They offer a large selection of Italian wines, which you can savour at the bar or in the underground restaurant. *Rynek Główny 13 | www.pasaz-13.pl*

CHILDREN

INSIDER TIP **BAJO** ⊙ (114 B6) (*ℳ D7*)
A cult address for eco-friendly wooden toys. The products range from tiny figures and cars to wooden horses and doll's prams. The Gruffalo toys are particularly amusing. *Ulica Grodzka 60 | bajo.eu*

BUKOWSKI ★ (114 B3) (*ℳ D5*)
A dream for teddy bear lovers! From floor to ceiling, 400 stuffed animals fill these wooden shelves and come in all sizes. *Mon–Sat 10am–7pm | Ulica Sienna 1 | galeriabukowski.pl*

ART GALLERIES

GALERIA GOŁOGÓRSKI
(114 B4) (*ℳ D6*)
The gallery run by the artist Marian Gołogórski specialises in modern Polish painting and sculptures made of metal, stone and glass. *Tue–Fri 4pm–8pm, Sat 11am–3pm | Ulica Grodzka 29 | www.golo gorski.com*

JAN FEJKIEL GALLERY (113 F4) (*ℳ D4*)
This gallery has the largest stock of modern Polish graphic art and drawings in the city. It places great importance on supporting young Krakow artists and organises many exhibitions. *Mon–Fri 11am–6pm, Sat 11am–3pm | Ulica Sław-kowska 14 | www.fejkielgallery.com*

FASHION

CLICK FASHION (112 C4) (*ℳ B4*)
With two locations, this store offers a tasteful selection of women's fashion

that's made right here in Krakow. You'll find many clothing's designs, ranging from modest to extraordinary. *Ulica Grodzka 32; Store in Kazimierz: Ulica Krakowska 14*

SIMPLE ★
You may never see someone in public wearing the clothing made and sold here. This is because only two or three pieces of each model are made. The women's fashion here is created by two Polish designers. Their pieces have a modern touch and include lovely summer dresses, evening dresses and elegant suits. Located in the *Galeria Kra-kowska*, the *Galeria Kazimierz* and in the *Bonarka City Center (Ulica Kamieńskie-go 11)* (121 E4) (*ℳ 0*). *www.simple-cp.com*

JEWELLERY

AMBRA STILE ⭐ (114 B5) *(🗺 D6)*
Italian silver jewellery with semi-precious stones, as well as jewellery with amber and locally made pieces – from cuff links to small ants and lizards with amber bodies. *Ulica Grodzka 45 | www.ambra stile.krakow.pl*

BLAZKO JEWELLERY (118 B3) *(🗺 F8)*
Here you'll find attactive silver jewellery with a black-and-white finish, a style that defines the hallmark of Grzegorz Błażko's gallery. *Ulica Józefa 11 | www.blazko.pl*

S&A (114 C3) *(🗺 D5)*
Here you'll find an array of jewellery, spoons, chess games and cuff links. The products offered are made from real natural amber and come with a certificate of authenticity. The jewellery made out of INSIDER TIP striped flint from Sandomierz makes for a very special souvenir. *Mon–Fri 9am–9pm, Sat 10am–9pm, Sat 10am–9pm | Ulica Sienna 1 | www.s-a.pl*

LOW BUDGET

A flea market is held every Sunday in the suburb of *Grzegórzki* (food market during the week). Here you will find all kinds of goods – from old radios to Meissen porcelain. *Ulica Grzegórzecka | tram 1 Hala Targowa.*

Reserved (Ulica Pawia 5 | Galeria Krakowska | www.reserved.com) sells young fashion along with inexpensive bags, shoes and costume jewellery. Sales are held several times a year with discounts of up to 70 per cent.

SHOES & BAGS

DE MEHLEM (114 B4) *(🗺 D6)*
Handmade bags and leather clothing have been sold in this shop since 1912. Also in stock are beautiful bags decorated with amber and made by the Polish company Batycki. *Ulica Grodzka 43 | www.demehlem.com*

GINO ROSSI (114 B3) *(🗺 D4)*
Trendy, Italian-style shoes and bags of the finest leather for all the family. *There are several branches, e.g. Ulica Szewska 4 | www.ginorossi.com*

WITTCHEN (119 E3) *(🗺 H7)*
Exclusive products made in Poland. Leather bags, cases, gloves, jackets, umbrellas and exquisite luggage. *Ulica Podgórska 34 | Galeria Kazimierz | www.wittchen.com*

SOUVENIRS

BROKAT (114 B3) *(🗺 D5)*
Here you'll find exquisite fabric item, like dolls, handmade cushions and tea cosies.Many of pieces are made by the students of the Krakow art academy. *Ulica Bracka 9*

ĆMIELÓW PORCELANA
(114 C6) *(🗺 E7)*
The largest producer of thin porcelain in Europe. A store that offers great sets and, for collectors, a small series of porcelain figures. *Ulica Stradomska 3 | www.porcelana.pl*

GALERIA (114 B5) *(🗺 D7)*
A place for many small souvenirs made by Krakow-based artists. Materials used include glass, ceramic, clay and wood. The hand-painted furniture is especially attractive. *Ulica Grodzka 60*

Much of the stuff at Grzegórzecka flea market takes you on a journey hrough time

SUKIENNICE (CLOTH HALL)
(114 B3) (*M D5*)

On Market Square, you'll find the largest selection of Krakow-made souvenirs ranging from jewellery and wooden articles to leather bags, traditional clothing, ceramics and glass articles. *Rynek Główny 2*

SPIRITS

REGIONALNE ALKOHOLE
(118 B2) (*M F7*)

Besides their large selection of international brands, this beautiful liquor store offers shelf after shelf full of regional beer, wines, spirits and vodka. *Mon–Thurs 10am–10pm, Fri/Sat 10am–midnight, Sun noon–9pm | Ulica Miodowa 28a | www.regionalnealkohole.com*

SZAMBELAN (114 B4) (*M D5*)

Liqueurs and vodkas, alongside vinegar and olive oil, in huge glass bottles from which you can draw off the desired quantity. Try the rose or orange and chocolate liqueurs as well. *Ulica Bracka 9 | www.szambelan.pl*

SWEETS

KRAKOWSKA MANUFAKTURA CZEKOLADY (114 E5) (*M D5*)

Production, sales outlet and café all rolled into one. You can watch as the pralines and chocolate bars are made. The chocolate dragons are a popular souvenir. *Ulica Grodzka 11 | chocolate.krakow.pl*

TORUŃSKIE PIERNIKI (114 B4) (*M D5*)

The famous gingerbread from Thorn coated with chocolate or with different coloured icing is available in all sizes. *Ulica Grodzka 14*

WEDEL ★ (114 B3) (*M D4*)

Traditional confectioners selling handmade pralines, chocolate and sweets. Two of their delicious specialities are *torcik wedlowski* (a gateau with layers of chocolate and nut cream) and *ptasie mleczko* (milk chocolate truffles filled with cream). You can sample the delicacies in the café next door. *Rynek Główny 46 | wedelpijalnie.pl*

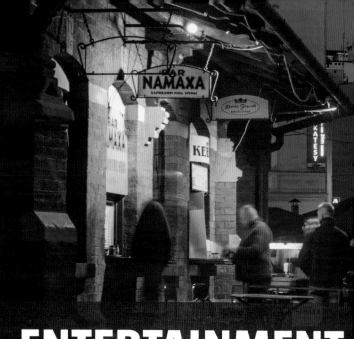

ENTERTAINMENT

CITY WHERE TO START?

Krakow's coolest jazz venues are below ground level in the medieval cellars, while the best clubs and pubs line the streets around **Rynek Główny**, most of them in the pedestrian precinct. Klezmer music is performed in many of the Jewish restaurants on **Ulica Szeroka** in **Kazimierz**. If you're looking for a night out on the town, **Plac Nowy** is the place to be for those wanting to party in the pubs or celebrate outdoors on the streets. Tram number 24 (Ulica Miodowa) takes you directly into the centre of Kazimierz's nightlife.

There are only a few cities in the world where the nightlife is as young, colourful and exciting as in Krakow. The best thing about Krakow, however, is its unique character as the people refuse to follow every international trend.

Kazimierz is dominated by everything unusual, alternative and artsy. No wonder students and artists love being here! You can party till dawn in the district's dimly lit cafés, clubs and pubs. Plac Nowy is surrounded by several old, partially renovated buildings and cellars. Inside you'll commonly find mismatched tables, antique sofas, cinema chairs, school desks, exhibitions by young artists, modern theatre and cabaret shows. The vibe around Kazimierz is always buzzing, guaranteeing a night full of fun and

Whether it's classical music, disco, jazz or klezmer, outdoors or in a Gothic cellar, Krakow knows how to have a good time

artistic encounters. Podgórze's nightlife is also growing, not to mention its cultural centre Tytano, located in a former tobacco factory just west of the Old Town. Here you'll find an array of shabby-chic pubs, clubs and bars, all boasting an industrial flair.

The nightlife in the city centre is often tamer than in the surrounding districts, but it also caters more often for tourists. In the Old Town, it is more likely that you will be asked for an ID or be turned away by a bouncer for not being properly dressed. Most clubs and pubs are best reached on foot and located in and around Rynek Główny. Most pubs are underground in beautifully renovated cellars, and many boast an inner courtyard or garden.

And then there's jazz – the music prevailing over the Old Town and its surrounding areas. Many jazz musicians live here for this reason, including the exceptional violinist Nigel Kennedy. In addition to his regular concerts at the Kraków Philharmonic, he often performs in the jazz clubs (and during klezmer concerts), as

DJs and turntables spinning records in Krakow: a modern trend

well. Many pubs and clubs don't serve just one purpose but are rather a music venue/restaurant/dance club. They just don't see a reason to separate these functions. Besides jazz, Krakow also boasts high culture: the Krakow Philharmonic Hall, many theatres, operas and classical music. Some events are even held outdoors or at select locations, like in the arcaded courtyard of the Wawel Castle or one of Krakow's many churches. Keep in mind that the churches are usually not heated so always be sure to bring a light pullover, even in summer.

Women usually don't have to pay an admission fee at the clubs. Men, however, are required to pay 20–30 Pln to get in. In most cases, everyone gets in the clubs for free after 1am. When you go out, only take the valuables and cash you need as the clubs tend to be packed with people at the weekend. Some clubs demand guests be 21 to enter, and there are strict rules to follow at all locations. If you're under 18, you're not allowed alcohol and cigarettes! Krakow also has lovely little

cinemas showing original films with Polish subtitles.

CLUBS & DISCO

BACCARAT MUSIC CLUB
(114 B4) (*Ⓜ D5*)
If you're looking for a nightclub with a fancy baroque style, you've come to the right place! Black and red leather sofas decorate the interior while, as it should be, dance and disco music dominate the club's sound system. *Fri/Sat 9pm–5am | Ulica Stolarska 13 | www.baccaratclub.pl*

FORUM PRZESTRZENIE
(117 E6) (*Ⓜ D10*)
This bistro/music club is a great spot to get the night rolling and a popular hang-out for artists. The food here is also good. Find a lounger outside and relax by the Vistula. Open-air concerts and exhibitions take place here often. *Daily 10am–4am | Ulica Marii Konopnickiej 28 | mob. 51434 29 39 | www.forumprzestrzenie.com*

red-and-blue neon lights. Very popular among young people who like dancing to music spun by exceptionally good DJs: funk, disco, electro, house. *Daily from 11pm | Plac Dominikański 6 | www.facebook.com/ProzakDwaZero*

SHINE CLUB (115 D5) *(𝄞 F6)*
Finally, a club suitable for that little black dress! This is one of the city's most famous nightclubs, boasting three bars and dance floors spread out over 1000 m² of space. As it used to be a cinema, the interior is royally furnished and impressively illuminated with LED lighting. Top DJs perform here and play house music, charts, hip-hop and R&B. *Fri/Sat 10pm–5pm | Ulica Starowislna 16 | www.shineclub.com.pl*

REAKTYWACJA (114 B4) *(𝄞 D6)*
Dance and music club in the cellar and on the first floor. People chill out here

JAZZ ROCK CAFE (114 B2) *(𝄞 D4)*
Don't let the name give you the wrong impression. This is actually a cult address for rock music! Get ready to rock out! Two rooms, two bars and a proper loud sound. Perfect for those wanting to lose themselves in the house music or see a live show. *Tue–Fri from 7pm | Sławkowska 12 | on Facebook*

POD JASZCZURAMI ●
(114 B3) *(𝄞 D5)*
Established in 1960, this is one of the city's oldest student clubs and translates as 'Among Lizards' in English. The building dates from medieval times and features a coat of arms above the entrance depicting two little green reptiles (hence the name). It's a café by day and a club by night (from 8pm) – concerts on Fridays, DJs on Saturdays, and karaoke on Thursdays and Sundays. *Daily from 9am | Rynek Główny 8 | www.podjaszczurami.pl*

PROZAK 2.0 (114 B–C4) *(𝄞 D5)*
A disco club in a traditional Krakow cellar! Three dance floors, four bars and

⭐ **Harris Piano Jazz Bar**
Jazz is jazz is jazz – in one of the city's most famous live music clubs → p. 70

⭐ **Piano Rouge**
It ist not only the interior that is luxurious. The music and Indian cuisine are also top class → p. 71

⭐ **Alchemia**
Krakow location with cult following in the epicentre of Kasimierzs pulsating nightlife → p. 72

⭐ **Filharmonia Krakowska im. Karola Szymanowskiego**
Symphonies, organ and jazz concerts: one of the best orchestras in the country has a virtuoso command of all styles of music → p. 73

MARCO POLO HIGHLIGHTS

Piano Rouge Bar: Sit back and let the live music ease your cares away!

every day, but they also dance to house and techno, and there are special events such as karaoke and reggae nights. During happy hour on Monday and Wednesday *(4–6pm)*, a large beer only costs 3 Pln. Do not go too casually dressed, otherwise the bouncer might not let you in! *Daily from 8pm | Ulica Grodzka 34 | www.reaktywacja.com.pl*

SPOŁEM (114 B2) (𝄇 D4)

A place where Poles find political nostalgia. Accompanied by a healthy dose of irony, this club takes you back in time with its Communist propaganda. They offer a wide selection of drinks, all cleverly named after terms relating to the Iron Curtain era. They play popular chart music and Polish music from the '80s and '90s. Weekends are packed. *Mon–Fri from 5pm, Sat/Sun from 6pm | Świętego Tomasza 4 | www.pub spolem.pl*

JAZZ

HARRIS PIANO JAZZ BAR ★ ●
(114 B3) *(𝄇 D4)*

One of the most famous jazz clubs in Krakow! Several live concerts take place here every week *(from 9pm)*: traditional jazz on Tuesday, a jam session on Thursday, Friday is blues night, and international jazz stars perform on Saturday *(Thu–Sat admission starts at 30 Pln, otherwise free entry)*. Good drinks and an excellent selection of beer are served at one of the longest bars in town. Pizza is available if you're hungry. *Sat/Sun from 10am, otherwise from 11am | Rynek Główny 28 | www. harris.krakow.pl*

U MUNIAKA (114 C3) *(𝄇 E4)*

A jazz club founded by saxophonist Janusz Muniak. Located in a brick cellar with arched ceilings, the club attracts a good mix of artists and musicians, and the atmosphere is superb. Live concerts take place at 9pm on several days during the week (see website). *Daily from 7pm | Ulica Floriańska 3 | jazzumuniaka.club*

PIANO ROUGE ★ (114 B3) *(ΩΩ D5)*
Red carpets, a chandelier and comfortable sofas. A plush, yet ideal environment for great live jazz concerts *(daily at 9pm)*. Burgers and other Italian/Polish specialities are also available. *Daily from 9.30am | Rynek Główny 46 | www.thepianorouge.com*

PIEC ART (114 B3) *(ΩΩ D4)*
No, you aren't seeing things. The bar has actually been built inside a massive, partly tiled oven. The bar's name, Piec, means 'oven' in Polish. Guests are served in a beautifully renovated Gothic cellar. A wide range of drinks and cocktails are available. On Wednesdays and Thursdays, live acts alternate between Polish jazz musicians and international stars. Concerts start at 8.30pm, and guests wine and dine at their tables during the show. Fish soup is their speciality. *Daily from noon | Ulica Szewska 21 | www.piecart.pl*

CINEMAS

ARS ●
Five auditoriums under a single roof, including a cinema café (Kiniarnia), in which you can order drinks from the bar during the film. Placed in an old ballroom, the *Reduta* is particularly beautiful. The films are shown in the original language. ARS closed in January 2019 but is planned to reopen. Check the website to find out when and where: *www.ars.pl*

POD BARANAMI (114 B3) *(ΩΩ D5)*
Three air-conditioned auditoriums located in a former palace on Market Square. The cinema organises INSIDER TIP▶ programmes on special themes several times each year. This might include a week of Spanish or African films, although the

TIME TO CHILL

City trips can be rather tiring, and it is, therefore, a good idea to take a break from time to time. A *paddle-boat tour on the Vistula (May–mid-Sept daily 10am to nightfall | 20–30 Pln/hour | Ulica Kościuszki 16)* **(116 B3)** *(ΩΩ B7)* has two wonderful effects: you will experience Krakow from a completely new perspective – and be able to really relax on the water on a warm, sunny day. Relaxation is also what ● *Kryspinów (admission fee 12 Pln, parking 10 Pln | www.kryspinow.com.pl | bus 209 Kryspinów Zalew)* **(121 D4)** *(ΩΩ O)* is all about. That is where you will be able to enjoy yourself swimming, rowing, windsurfing or just splashing around in the artificial lakes in the countryside only 12 km/11 mi west of Krakow on the A4. And the ● *Farmona Wellness & Spa* **(121 E5)** *(ΩΩ O) (Tue–Sun 9am–9pm | Ulica Jugowicka 10c | tel. 12 252 70 20 | www.spakrakow.pl | bus 244 Jugowicka)* in the hotel of the same name is a genuine feel-good oasis. Regardless of whether you are alone or with a partner, you will be pampered all day long with special treatments from Bali and Hawaii: massages with hot stones and fragrant oils followed by aromatic baths.

main focus is on European cinema. There's a small café on the first floor. The films are screened in the original language. *Rynek Główny 27 | Pałac Pod Baranami | www.kinopodbaranami.pl*

PUBS & INNS

ALCHEMIA ⭐ (118 B3) (*𝄞 F8*)
Cult pub in Kazimierz: there is a stuffed crocodile hanging over the bar and guests enter the next room through a cupboard. Inside this candle-lit bar with bare walls, guests sit on rickety chairs at old tables. The drinks are great, but and the apple pie is sensational. Concerts and modern theatre events take place in the cellar. Outside, guests are seated in the heart of Kazimierz, and it's a fine place to watch the youth bar hop between the pubs on Plac Nowy. *Daily from 10am | Ulica Estery 5 | www.alchemia.com.pl*

OMERTA PUB & MORE
(118 B3) (*𝄞 F8*)
A poster above this bar read 'Join the Corleone Family'. Even if you choose not to be a member, you're still welcome to try beers from all over the world. They serve INSIDER**TIP** over 30 beers on tap and 150 bottled craft beers. Evenings are packed, so *call to make a reservation. Daily from 4pm | Ulica Warszauera 3 | Ulica Kupa 3 | tel. 5 01 50 82 27 | on Facebook*

PROPAGANDA (118 B2) (*𝄞 E7*)
This is the place for you if you want to feel a real Communist atmosphere: Lenin greets the guests from posters on the walls. Other parts of the wall are covered in socialist-style signs. A host of great drinks. You absolutely must try INSIDER**TIP** the speciality *wściekły pies*: the ice-cold rectified spirit with tabasco and raspberry juice really is something special. *Daily from noon | Ulica Miodowa 20*

PUB POD ZIEMIĄ (118 C2) (*𝄞 F7*)
Enjoy rock, metal and alternative music in this small cellar pub in Kazimierz. Plenty of delicious drinks are offered. Concerts take place on the weekend and are followed by a night of karaoke. Ladies are treated to cheaper prices on Wednesday. *Mon–Sat from 4pm, Sun from 5pm | Ulica Miodowa 43 | pubpodziemia.pl*

LE SCANDALE ● (118 B3) (*𝄞 F8*)
Why not stay for the whole day?! Come for breakfast and stay for burgers, steaks and pizza later. You'll need the energy when night falls. Hang out at the bar or in the pub's beautiful inner courtyard. The DJ's music keeps everything in motion. *Daily from 8am | Plac Nowy 9 | on Facebook*

SINGER (118 B3) (*𝄞 F8*)
Nomen est omen: old Singer sewing machines have been turned into the tables of this, the oldest, pub in Kazimierz. In summer you can also sit outside in the fresh air; fine selection of alcoholic drinks, as well as coffee and cake. *Daily from 10am | corner of Ulica Izaaka/Estery*

LOW BUDGET

In most of the *Krakow clubs*, women do not have to pay an admission fee – or only a reduced one; ● late at night, it is usually free for all.

Many pubs and clubs have *happy-hour days* (often on Monday) when beer is extremely inexpensive.

Enjoy a night in good taste at Alchemia – a trendy place

WARSZTAT (118 B3) *(ⓜ F8)*

A mixture of café and pub. The biggest impression is made by the interior decoration with all the old musical instruments: a piano has been inserted upright into the bar! This is where the way-out in-crowd meets in Kazimierz. There is music in the background: blues, jazz or klezmer, and the beer is served in enormous jugs. *Daily from 10am | Ulica Izaaka 3 | www. restauracjawarsztat.pl*

OPERA & CLASSICAL MUSIC

FILHARMONIA KRAKOWSKA IM. KAROLA SZYMANOWSKIEGO ⭐ (114 A4) *(ⓜ C5)*

The Krakow Philharmonic Society was founded in 1909 and has had its home in this neo-Baroque building since 1930. The Krakow Radio Symphony and Philharmonic Orchestras are two of the best in Poland. Symphonic and organ concerts are held in this hall as are jazz performances and other concerts as part of various festivals. Programme in English.

The Philharmonic also organises the **INSIDER TIP** *Wawel Evenings (Wieczory wawelskie)*, where chamber music is played in the fabulous atmosphere inside the castle or its arcaded courtyard. *Ticket office: Tue–Fri 11am–2pm and 3–5pm, Sat/Sun one hour before the performance | Ulica Zwierzyniecka 1 | www. filharmonia.krakow.pl*

OPERA KRAKOWSKA (115 F1) *(ⓜ H3)*

The multicoloured, segmented complex which houses the opera is the backdrop to traditional and modern productions of Polish and international operas. The **INSIDER TIP** Summer Festival is very popular; performances are held in the arcaded courtyard of Wawel Castle as well as in the opera house itself. **INSIDER TIP** Early booking of tickets is an absolute must! *Ticket office: Mon–Fri 10am–7pm, Sat noon–7pm, Sun two hours before the performance | five price categories between 30 and 120 Pln | Ulica Lubicz 48 | www. opera.krakow.pl*

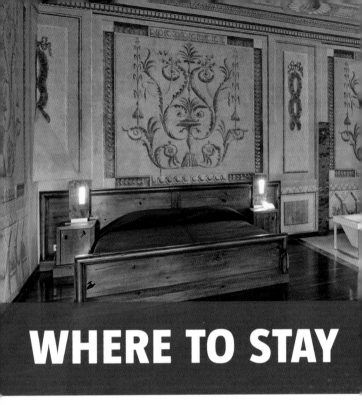

WHERE TO STAY

Although you're welcome to book a room at one of the international hotel chains in the city, you're better off staying in an accommodation equally as eccentric as Krakow, all boasting individually furnished rooms.

It's true that family guest houses in Krakow don't always offer the highest standards of luxury, but the atmosphere here is especially welcoming. You'll find plenty of reasonably priced hotels, guest houses and private accommodation in Kazimierz. The cheapest hotels are frequently located far away from the city centre in buildings dating back to the 1960s and 1970s. Therefore, rather than booking a room at a one or two-star hotel on the outskirts of town, we recommend staying at a nicer hostel or guest house in a more

central location. You may not be served your meals in the morning, but many of these offer a dining room where guests can prepare their own breakfast.

The best (and more expensive) hotels are located right in the centre in the pedestrian precinct, and most are in Gothic or Renaissance townhouses and palaces. Each accommodation has its own history, metaphorically painted on beautiful wooden ceilings, Gothic portals and fresco-covered walls. Although historical, these hotels are nonetheless modern, offering tech-savvy facilities and exceptional comfort. Next door to these luxurious hotels, however, you'll also find many moderately priced hotels that are well-furnished and equally comfortable. In short, regardless of whether the place

Stylish luxury hotels, Gothic townhouses, modern family hotels and cosy guest rooms – rarely do cities offer so much variety!

is comparatively new, a few years old, well-established or newly renovated, the accommodations in Krakow have been meeting international standards for a long time.

No matter where you decide to stay, always ask if they have any special offers as there are often price reductions if you book a room for several nights. You'll also frequently come across special weekend rates, family offers and hotel packages which include city tours or museum passes. It's also worth taking a look at their websites as some hotels offer up to 30 per cent off online bookings. If you're looking for the best deal possible, come to Krakow during the off-season when booking prices are often 50 per cent lower. The high season starts with Easter and lasts until the end of October. If you want to find the best deal on luxury houses, visit *www.booking.com* and *www.venere.com*. For hotels or holiday flats, two good addresses to check out are *www.krakow-hotel-guide.com* and *www.staypoland.com*.

The delightful inner courtyard of the Hotel Copernicus exudes history

HOTELS: EXPENSIVE

HOTEL COPERNICUS ☆
(114 B5) (⌀ D6)

Fancy a room with a view of the Royal Castle in a listed building from the 16th century? Then this is the place for you! This hotel was lovingly renovated with great attention paid to each detail. The rooms are all individually designed and some have had the original Gothic and Renaissance murals restored in them. The hotel is in a very quiet area. **INSIDER TIP** The most beautiful rooms offer a view of Ulica Kanonicza. The rooftop terrace also boasts a spectacular view. In the cellar, you'll find a stylish spa and pool. Book online to get up to 30 per cent off the price. *29 rooms | Ulica Kanonicza 16 | tel. 1 24 24 34 00 | www.copernicus.hotel. com.pl*

GRAND HOTEL (114 B2) (⌀ D4)

A hotel that lives up to its name! Established in 1887, this luxury hotel was once the palace of Princess Marcelina Czartoryska. Many of the rooms are equipped with tiled stoves, old parquet flooring and 16th-century wall paintings. The Duchess Suite, once Marcelina's private salon, boasts a 16th-century wooden ceiling on which gorgeous cupids are painted. Four restaurants, cafés and bars. *65 rooms | double rooms from 900 Pln | Ulica Sławkowska 5/7 | tel. 1 24 24 08 00 | www.grand.pl*

GRÓDEK (114 C3) (⌀ E5)

A hotel in a Gothic building in a peaceful location in the heart of town. Each room has a different interior design; the Gothic church floor in the reception area was saved during renovations and laid here. There is a lovely view of the Old

Town from the charming restaurant; the library has a wide selection of books. Objects found during renovation work are displayed in the hotel, in INSIDER TIP Poland's only private archaeological museum. *23 rooms | Ulica Na Gródku 4 | tel. 124 31 90 30 | www.donimirski.com*

OSTOYA PALACE (112 C6) *(ω B5)*

This stylish hotel, decorated with antique furniture, is located in the renovated, listed Ostaszewski Palace from 1895. It was built by Józef Pokutyński, one of Krakow's best architects. Many details, such as wall paintings and stucco work, have been preserved over the years. If you want to sleep in a really big bed (2 m × 2 m/6.6 ft × 6.6 ft), book one of the suites. *23 rooms | Ulica Józefa Piłsudkiego 24 | tel. 124 30 90 00 | www.ostoyapalace.pl*

PAŁAC BONEROWSKI ★
(114 B3) *(ω D4)*

Luxurious rooms and suites in a 16th-century castle in a top location directly on the Market Square. Many details, including portals, wooden ceilings and murals, have been preserved. The restaurant *Bonerowska Steak & Fish* serves European cuisine and *St. John Jazz & Wine Club* offers drinks and music in an elegantly designed cellar. The INSIDER TIP Chopin concerts in the evening can be attended by guests and the public. *16 rooms | Ulica św. Jana 1 | tel. 123 74 13 00 | www.palacbonerowski.pl*

POD RÓŻĄ ★ (114 C2) *(ω E4)*

The oldest hotel in Krakow: even Honoré de Balzac laid his head here. The original architecture of the 15th-century townhouse on the Royal Way was combined with the luxury and comfort of the 21st century to create this hotel. Fine restaurant with a large wine cellar. *57 rooms |*

Ulica Floriańska 14 | tel. 124 24 33 00 | www.hotel.com.pl

HOTELS: MODERATE

HOTEL ALEF (118 A3) *(ω E8)*

This hotel in Kazimierz has 35 comfortable, but simply appointed, rooms. The main attraction is the staircase that the owner has turned into an art gallery. There is also a restaurant serving traditional Jewish food. *Ulica św. Agnieszki 5 | tel. 124 24 31 31 | www.alefhotel.pl*

ATRIUM HOTEL (114 C1) *(ω E3)*

This modern, centrally located hotel was renovated just a few years ago. The rooms are simply furnished and there

---

MARCO POLO HIGHLIGHTS

★ **Pałac Bonerowski**
What more could you ask for: staying in a castle with a view of St Mary's Church and dining on Japanese delicacies under a glass roof → p. 77

★ **Pod Różą**
Would you like to sleep in the same room as Balzac? Nothing is impossible in Krakow's oldest hotel → p. 77

★ **Stary**
Europe's most beautiful hotel also has the most beautiful view of the city from its rooftop terrace → p. 78

★ **Antique Apartments**
Complete with a substantial feel-good factor: beautiful flats in a stylishly restored historic house in the centre – at a fair price, too → p. 81

are also two apartments with kitchenettes. *52 rooms | Ulica Krzywa 7 | tel. 124 30 02 03 | www.hotelatrium.com.pl*

APARTAMENTY BRACKA 6
(114 B4) (*ω D5*)
The apartments and studios in this 500-year-old townhouse in a prime location have been renovated with painstaking care. They all have parquet floors and air-conditioning and some have a balcony. The rooms are equipped with a small kitchenette and wireless Internet access. *8 flats | Ulica Bracka 6 | tel. 123 41 40 11 | www.bracka6.pl*

APARTAMENTY PARKSIDE KRAKÓW
(115 D3) (*ω F5*)
A stylish hotel consisting of two 19th-century buildings connected by a landscaped courtyard. The hotel is just 500 m/550 yd from Market Square, and most rooms feature either a balcony, loggia or terrace

in the garden. Some even come with a hot tub. *30 rooms and apartments | Ulica Mikołaja Kopernika 8 | tel. 725 55 05 56 | www.parksidekrakow.pl*

ELEKTOR HOTEL (114 C2) (*ω E4*)
Located in the heart of the Old Town, this newly renovated hotel offers stylishly furnished rooms in a beautiful tenement house. Special offers and packages are always available. If you book one room, for example, the second one is only 1 Pln and the third night is free! There's a great Sicilian restaurant in the hotel, so there's no need to dine out. *21 rooms | Ulica Szpitalna 28 | tel. 124 23 23 17 | www.hotelelektor.pl*

ESTER (118 C3) (*ω F8*)
This hotel is located in the heart of Kazimierz with a view of the old synagogues. The rooms have very tasteful antique-style furniture. *15 rooms | Ulica Szeroka*

MORE THAN A GOOD NIGHT'S SLEEP

If Heaven were a Hotel...
Once upon a time, there was an old, 16th-century townhouse chosen to be the most beautiful hotel in all of Europe. Granted, this happened quite some time ago, but the ☆ Stary Hotel **(114 B2)** (*ω D4*) (*78 rooms | double rooms from 800 Pln | Ulica Szczepańska 5 | tel. 123 84 08 08 | www.stary.hotel.com.pl*) *is still a dream to stay in and affordable at that!* Checking in here is like going back in time, but with all the modern amenities! Excellent comfort: dark wooden furniture, silk curtains, rare wooden and colourful marble bathrooms. Then there's the city view

from the rooftop café's terrace – just heavenly!

Red Bricks and Wood
It's possible that Hostel Luneta Warszawska **(102 C3)** (*ω F1*) (*15 rooms | Ulica Kamienna 16 | tel. 124 44 63 65 | www.lunetahostel.pl*) *is the most beautiful one in Krakow. After all, it's located in a beautifully renovated fortification from the 19th century. It's a red brick fortress boasting rustic wooden floors both in the lobby and the rooms. Book a room with a personal bathroom or stay in an 8-person room. The terrace has purposely been left unrenovated. It's beautiful just the way it is!*

Hotel Pollera – a place to experiece history in style!

20 | tel. 124 26 11 88 | www.hotel-ester.
krakow.pl

FLORYAN (114 C2) (*∅ E4*)
The rooms in this 16th-century town-house are rather modern and not particularly fancy but they are decently equipped and the location is perfect. Hotel guests get a 10 per cent reduction on meals in the *Vesuvius Restaurant*. *35 rooms | Ulica Floriańska 38 | tel. 124 311418 | www.floryan.com.pl*

MATEJKO (114 C1) (*∅ E3*)
Not far away from the railway station in a renovated residential building. Spacious rooms with modern fittings. Good (albeit not particularly quiet) location. *48 rooms | Plac Jana Matejki 8 | tel. 124 22 47 37 | www.matejkohotel.pl*

POD WAWELEM ☆ (114 A5) (*∅ C7*)
A hotel offering small, modern rooms that are sometimes decorated in rather bright colours. Ask for a room with a bal-cony and a view of the Vistula. The restaurant and café on the roof have a wonderful view towards Wawel Castle and over the river. The hotel is only a five-minute walk from the Rynek Główny. Free bike rental! *48 rooms | Plac na Groblach 22 | tel. 124 26 26 26 | www.hotel podwawelem.pl*

POLESKI ☆ (117 D3) (*∅ C8*)
This modern hotel scores with its high standards. During the summer, there is a restaurant with a unique view of the castle on the roof. The Classic Panorama rooms with a view of the Vistula and to-wards the Wawel are especially lovely. *20 rooms | Ulica Sandomierska 6 | tel. 122 60 54 05 | www.hotelpoleski.pl*

POLLERA (114 C2) (*∅ E4*)
This magnificent house built in 1834 has now been turned into a hotel, in which you can feel the special atmosphere of times gone by. The INSIDER TIP stained-glass windows in the staircase created

Majestic façade and fair prices: Hotel Royal

correspondingly high standard. Perfect location opposite St Florian's Gate, in middle of the Old Town, yet in the quiet pedestrian precinct. The suites with their antique-style furnishings are especially beautiful. *54 rooms | Ulica Pijarska 17 | tel. 124 22 11 44 | donimirski.com/en*

HOTELS: BUDGET

APARTHOTEL PERGAMIN
(113 F2) *(𝄞 D3)*
Very tastefully furnished rooms and apartments in an ideal location. Plenty of wood plus bare brick elements make for a stylish contrast to the modern, luxury feel. Enjoy a 15 per cent discount when staying three or more nights. Three additional locations listed on their website. *31 rooms | Ulica Długa 26 | tel. 126 30 91 65 | www.premium-hotels.pl*

ATELIER APARTHOTEL (115 F1) *(𝄞 G3)*
Pleasant, reasonably-priced accommodation in 2, 3 or 4-bed rooms is on offer at this hotel. You're close to the main railway station and not far from the city centre. Extra charge for a private car park, but breakfast is included. *27 rooms | Ulica Topolowa 40 | tel. 124 23 21 21 | www.arteryhotels.pl*

CAMPANILE (114 C3) *(𝄞 E5)*
Part of a hotel chain in an ideal spot just a few minutes from the Market Square, directly on the green belt. *106 rooms | Ulica św. Tomasza 34 | tel. 124 24 26 00 | www.campanile.com*

DOM CASIMI (118 C3) *(𝄞 F8)*
Modern guest rooms in the middle of Kazimierz. Simply equipped, but bright and cheerful. Everything is new and of good quality, and you can also hire bicycles. *12 rooms | Ulica Szeroka 7/8 | tel. 124 26 11 93 | www.casimi.pl*

by Stanisław Wyspiański bring back memories of art nouveau days. Thick red and green carpets, comfortable sofas and Tiffany-style lamps make the flair of this exceptional house complete. The suites are exceptionally beautiful. *40 rooms | Ulica Szpitalna 30 | tel. 124 22 10 44 | www.pollera.com.pl*

HOTEL POLSKI POD BIAŁYM ORŁEM
(114 C2) *(𝄞 E4)*
This establishment has been in the possession of the Czartoryskis – a Polish aristocratic family – since 1913 and is of a

PIANO GUESTHOUSE (U C2) (*𝄞 F1*)

A family guest house with colourfully painted antique furniture. It's not far from Rakowicki Cemetery. In summer, breakfast is served out on the terrace, located in the middle of a beautiful garden. You don't need to pay for a transfer ticket when travelling here from central station. *7 rooms | Ulica Kątowa 4 | tel. 6 98 35 06 48 | www. pianoguesthouse.pl*

INSIDER TIP **HOTEL ROYAL**
(114 B6) (*𝄞 D7*)

As cheap as this hotel is, it couldn't be better situated. It's located at the foot of Wawel Castle, making it one of the city's most frequented hotels offered at this price. They also have special offers and a small wellness area for guests. Booking is best done over the phone. *99 rooms | Ulica św. Gertrudy 26–29 | tel. 126 21 35 00 | www.hotelewam.pl*

APARTMENTS

ANTIQUE APARTMENTS ★
(114 B2) (*𝄞 D4*)

These two fantastically renovated historic houses in the city centre contain pleasantly furnished apartments of between 215 and 1450 ft² and include bathroom and free wi-fi. Enjoy a sumptuous breakfast at the restaurant *Scandale Royal* on the ground floor with its view of beautiful Szczepański Square (extra charge). Reception is open 24 hours a day. INSIDER TIP Lots of value-for-money offers if you book online. *58 apartments | Plac Szczepański 2/9 | tel. 124 30 21 67 | www.antiqueapartments. com*

APARTAMENTY KRAKÓW

The best choice for apartments in Krakow. The 434 flats are in the centre, on the Wawel or in Kazimierz, and each is fully equipped. No reception: once you've booked and paid online you meet the proprietor at the flat to collect the keys. *mob. 5 02 57 16 06 | apartament-krakow.pl*

OLD CITY APARTMENTS

Though these 30 different apartments are all marketed under the same name, they each have their own style and atmosphere. Located in the centre of Krakow, what they do have in common is modern furnishing and state-of-the-art technology. The apartments in the 'Gothic' series with their unplastered walls will transport you back to the Middle Ages, while the *kiążęcy* ('princely') category offers pure luxury with antique furniture. *mob. 0606 94 14 83 | www.oldcityapartments.eu*

LOW BUDGET

Students and young travellers under 30 who have ISIC or EURO<26 cards often enjoy reduced prices – not only in hotels but also in museums. *www.isic.de, euro26.pl/en*

You can stay in a room for eight to ten guests in the *Rynek7Hostel* (*Rynek Główny 7/6 | tel. 124 31 16 98 | www.hostelrynek7.pl*) for 45 Pln a night – and that includes a view of the Cloth Hall. An address for those who prefer to party more than sleep. Also double rooms.

You can find inexpensive accommodation in Krakow under *www.hostel. pl* and *www.krakow30.com*

DISCOVERY TOURS

① KRAKOW AT A GLANCE

START: ① Rynek Główny (Market Square)
END: ⑮ Plac Nowy (New Square)

1 day
Walking time
2.5 hours

Distance:
🚌 10 km/6.2 mi

COSTS: Admission fees and ⑨ carriage ride: about 170 Pln; ⑩ Wavelo bike sharing system: 10 Pln to register, 0.16 Pln/min to ride; Food and drink: 210 Pln

This tour introduces you to the historic heart of Krakow and its most important sights and lets you immerse yourself in the everyday life in the city. Mostly on foot, but also by horse-drawn carriage and water tram, the tour takes you on to Kazimierz, where you explore the Jewish part of the city and discover some beautiful places to relax and shop.

Would you like to explore the places that are unique to this city? Then the Discovery Tours are just the thing for you – they include terrific tips for stops worth making, breathtaking places to visit, selected restaurants and fun activities. It's even easier with the Touring App: download the tour with map and route to your smartphone using the QR Code on pages 2/3 or from the website address in the footer below – and you'll never get lost again even when you're offline.

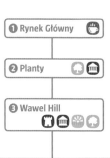

TOURING APP

→ p. 2/3

08:00am Start the day with breakfast on the main square
① Rynek Główny → p. 33 at **Café Noworolski** → p. 54, a place harking back to Krakow's imperial and royal past. **When you're ready, stroll along Ulica Sienna, and turn right through the landscaped ②** Planty Park → p. 33, **walking for 15 minutes until you reach the Wawel.**

09:00am You're now standing in front of **③** Wawel Hill → p. 41, the former seat of the Polish kings. Visit **Wawel Cathedral** → p. 36 and the **Royal Castle** → p. 41. You'll

① Rynek Główny ☕

② Planty ☕ 🏛

③ Wawel Hill 🎭 🏛 ❋ 🌳

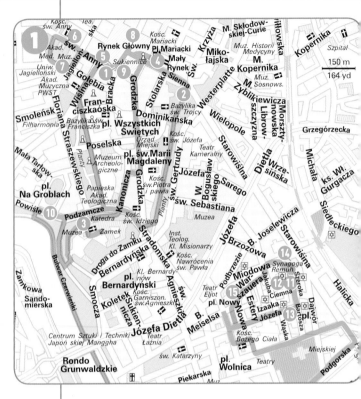

have a magnificent view over the city and River Vistula and the city from **Sigismund Tower**. **Leave the hill via the Dragon's Cave → p. 40 and head to the river to find the Wawel Dragon Statue → p. 40.**

11:15am Take a 45-minute walk back to Rynek Główny to discover a real masterpiece! Make your way into **④ St Mary's Church → p. 31** to find the world-famous **Veit Stoss Altarpiece → p. 31** which can be visited during renovation. After exploring the ins and outs of this splendid Gothic basilica, head up one of its newly renovated **towers** and take in one of the most beautiful views of the city.

④ St Mary's Church

01:45pm Every hour, **St Mary's Trumpet Call → p. 16** can be heard from the highest tower. Listen in while stopping for a snack break at **⑤ Café Szał → p. 34, located en route to the Cloth Hall, just a short walk away.**

⑤ Café Szał

02:30pm Having got your strength up again, turn **into Ulica św. Anny at the southwest corner of Rynek Główny behind the Town Hall tower. Follow the street until you come to the magnificent baroque ⑥ Church of St Anne** → p. 32 towering up on your right. **To the left is the University building.** A visit to the museum in the **⑦ Collegium Maius** → p. 30 will whisk you back to the Middle Ages. Don't miss the **carillon** → p. 30 in the university's inner courtyard at 3pm.

03:30pm From the heights of academia, the tour now leads you underground: **the exhibition entitled ⑧ Rynek Underground** → p. 35 **in the Cloth Hall** → p. 34 lets you walk through the city's exposed medieval streets. Back at ground level once more, the next stage of your journey back in time is about to begin. **Starting on Rynek Główny you embark on a ⑨ carriage ride** → p. 105 back into the middle of the fin-de-siècle era of the 19th century. **You travel along Ulica Grodzka and past the Franciscan Church** → **p. 30 and the Church of Saints Peter and Paul** → **p. 38. After 30 minutes you reach the oldest street in the city,** Ulica Kanonicza → p. 40, with its splendid **episcopal palaces. Now pass Wawel Hill to your right and keep going until your reach Ulica Powiśle** where you'll find **⑩ Wavelo,** a bike rental system. **Rent a bike and cruise along the Vistula until you reach the Father Bernatek Footbridge where you'll turn left onto the less busy Ulica Podgórska.**

04:30pm **Turn left at the next junction and hand in your bike at the rental station on Św. Wawrzyńca. You're now in the heart of the former Jewish town of** Kazimierz → p. 42. **Walk along Ulica Szeroka, past the Synagoga Stara** → p. 45 and stop at the **⑪ Old Jewish Cemetery** → p. 44 to take in the beautiful old tombstones. **Adjacent to the cemetery is the ⑫ Remuh Synagogue** → p. 44; take a look round the inside. The **shop is also worth a visit for souvenirs,** Jewish music and literature. **The long ⑬ Ulica Józefa** → p. 60 is directly ahead of you and is lined with small but interesting shops and galleries, such as **Szalom** or vintage and jewellery stores, like **Blazko Jewellery** → p. 64. Before you leave this street, loaded down with hand-crafted, unique souvenirs, **have a look at the inner courtyard of the house at** Ulica Józefa 12, where scenes from the film 'Schindler's List' were filmed. **After crossing the courtyard, turn right into Ulica Meiselsa.**

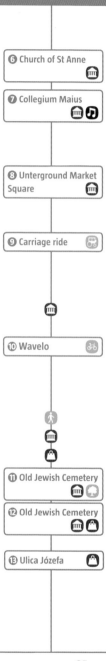

⑥ Church of St Anne

⑦ Collegium Maius

⑧ Unterground Market Square

⑨ Carriage ride

⑩ Wavelo

⑪ Old Jewish Cemetery

⑫ Old Jewish Cemetery

⑬ Ulica Józefa

⑭ Klezmer Hois 🍴🎵

⑮ Plac Nowy 🛍️🎵

07:00pm Stroll back once more to the Remuh Synagogue; the ⑭ **Klezmer Hois** → p. 58 is close by. Enjoy some Jewish specialities and, if you're lucky, INSIDER**TIP** listen to a klezmer concert. As you are in one of the city's trendiest districts, take in the nightlife **around the bustling ⑮ Plac Nowy** → p. 43 and head to the bar **Alchemia** → p. 72 – a cult favourite!

2
CONTRASTING DISTRICTS: KLEPARZ AND NOWA HUTA

START: ❶ Jama Michalika
END: ⓫ Szara

1 day
Walking time
2.5 hours

Distance:
🚋 21 km/13 mi

COSTS: Admission fee: 23 Pln; Tram: 10 Pln; Food: 150 Pln

IMPORTANT TIPS: The ❼ Archaeological Museum is closed on Saturdays.

Get away from the tourists in Kleparz, and spend a morning like the locals do. Visit a famous food market and then Nowa Huta – a former model communist city.

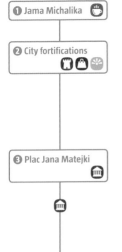

❶ Jama Michalika ☕

❷ City fortifications 🏛️🏰🌸

❸ Plac Jana Matejki 🏛️

🏛️

10:00am Start the day **at the** ❶ Jama Michalika → p. 54 café, one of the most famous art nouveau eateries in the city. **Following Ulica Florianska** takes you to the remains of the ❷ **city fortifications** → p. 28. **On the left-hand side** artists have hanged their paintings on the wall, thus creating a small open-air gallery. These works are also for sale. **Before passing through St Florian's Gate and entering Kleparz, climb up the Barbican** → p. 29 and take a look at the actual city of Krakow.

For many years, Kleparz was allowed to deteriorate; now things have taken a turn for the better. **You are now standing on** ❸ **Plac Jana Matejki (Matejko Square)** with the huge **Tannenberg Memorial** and the fine neo-Renaissance home of the **Krakow Art Academy** *(Plac Matejki 13)* which was built in 1880. **St Florian's Church at the other end of the square** is also worth a visit – this is where the career of Karol Wojtyła, later to become Pope John Paul II, began.

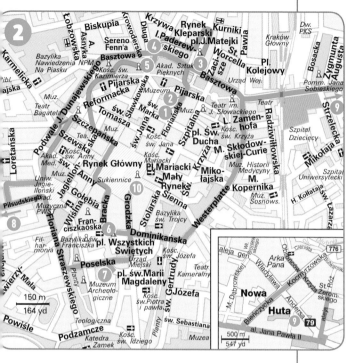

Go back to Matejko Square and turn into Ulica Paderewskiego. The largest ❹ **food market** *(in summer daily 9am–6pm, in winter until 4pm | Plac Kleparski)* in the heart of the city now lies before you. Here you can purchase virtually anything: fruit and vegetables, of course, plus cheese from Zakopane, ham and bread – it's not uncommon for farmers' wives to travel over 100 km/62 mi to sell the fruits of their labours here. Stop at INSIDER TIP **stand number 33** to stock up on provisions to take with you for your picnic later on: home-made hummus, organic fruit juices, sea buckthorn jam, sandwiches and coffee.

12:00pm The landscaped ❺ **Planty Park → p. 33 is directly in front of you** and encircles the city. It boasts an interesting open-air exhibition of 19th and 20th-century sculptures. **Stroll through the park** and stop for a picnic with your market purchases. After your meal, **carry on past the baroque Church of St Casimir the Prince until you reach** the ❻ **Franciscan Monastery → p. 30.** Pop in here to see

❹ Food market

❺ Planty

❻ Franciscan Monastery

Plenty of room for cyclists on Rynek Glowny

the delightful stained-glass windows made by Stanislaw Wyspiański, an outstanding artistic talent who decisively influenced Krakow during the fin-de-siècle era. We'll come back to him later.

Get ready to enter another world **at Ulica Senacka 3**, the **❼ Archaeological Museum** *(Jan–June Mon, Wed, Fri, Sun 9am–3pm, Tue, Thu 9am–6pm, July, Aug Sun–Fri 10am–5pm, Sept–Dec Sun–Fri 9am–3pm | admission 10 Pln)*. While here, you'll run into mummies and uncover other treasures from ancient Egypt. **Back to present day, you'll walk through Planty Park again and along Ulica Straszewskiej. On Józefa Piłsudskiego, enter the main building of the National Museum → p. 47 where you'll once again be able to study the works of** Stanislaw Wyspiański. After your visit, make time for a snack at **❽ Tribeca Coffee → p. 47, conveniently located in the same building**.

Afterwards, **continue along Szczepański Square, past the art nouveau Palace of Fine Arts and the Bunker of Arts,** which has made a name for itself with provocative contemporary exhibitions. **Back into the Planty, turn left and head for the tram stop Teatr Bagatela for the ride to Nowa Huta.**

03:30pm A totally different Krakow lies in store for you in **❾ Nowa Huta → p. 48**, the Socialist workers' town. **Get off the tram at the Plac Centralny → p. 48 and walk down the Aleja Róż → p. 48** through the attractive, generously proportioned part of Nowa Huta with its neo-classicist houses from the 1950s and 1960s. **Turn to the left down Ulica Stefana Żeromskiego and continue straight ahead as far as the Ark of the Lord → p. 48.** Inside, it's worth taking some time to explore and appreciate the modern interior of this church and its particularly impressive bronze sculpture of Christ.

07:00pm Take the **tram back to the city centre.** The **❿ Szara → p. 57** restaurant located in a medieval townhouse provides the perfect contrast, also in culinary terms. And seeing as you have done so much walking today, you deserve to treat yourself to a nightcap in the separate bar.

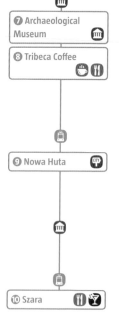

❼ Archaeological Museum

❽ Tribeca Coffee

❾ Nowa Huta

❿ Szara

3

IN THE KINGS' GARDEN

START: ① Le Scandale	1 day
END: ⑩ Piec Art	Driving time
Distance:	2.5 hours
🚲 35 km/22 mi	

COSTS: Bike hire for 1 day: 60–100 Pln; Taxi: about 30 Pln; Massage at ⑨ Farmona Wellness & Spa: from 200 Pln; Food: 130 Pln

IMPORTANT TIPS: At ② Krk Bike Rental → p. 101, rent a mountain bike or e-bike if you're not certain; they'll be inclines in Wolski Forest. Book in advance at ⑨ Farmona Wellness & Spa.

This bike tour takes you past churches and monasteries, through a picturesque and exclusive residential area and out into the countryside to the still unspoilt reaches of Wolski Forest.

09:00am Start with a hearty breakfast at ① **Le Scandale** *(Plac Szczepański 2)*. Next, rent an e-bike at ② **Krk Bike Rental** → p. 101 as the tour will be hilly. Before you get started, make **a detour to the** ③ **Biedronka** *(Rynek Główny 34)* supermarket to stock up on refreshments for the day. **Then ride through the Old Town and via Ulica Grodzka past the Wawel and continue along the Vistula.** The district of ④ **Zwierzyniec (Zoo)** includes the former hunting grounds and gardens of the Polish kings and the estates of the **Klasztor Norbertanek (Convent of the Premonstratensian Nuns)** and the **Church of St Augustine and John the Baptist** *(Ulica Kościuszki 88)*, **which you reach after about 10 minutes** (not open to the public).

You now turn off to the right and cross over the road. On your left you'll see a rare example of sacred wooden architecture: the **Kościół św. Małgorzaty (Church of St Margaret)** *(Ulica św. Bronisławy 3)*, originally built in the 17th century. Architecture of the 19th and early 20th centuries nestling in spacious parkland dominates this particular residential suburb of Krakow. **Turn left** into the particularly pretty INSIDERTIP **Ulica Gontyny.** **The route now takes you uphill into the Aleja Waszyngtona. Soon, on the right-hand side,** one of the oldest churches in the city comes into view, the **Kościół Najśw. Salwatora (Church of the Redeemer)** *(Ulica św. Bronisławy 9)*. **As you continue along the chestnut-lined avenue, you pass the** ⑤ **Sal-**

① Le Scandale 🚲

② Krk Bike Rental

③ Biedronka 🛒

④ Zwierzyniec 🐾 🏛

⑤ Salwator Cemetery 🏛

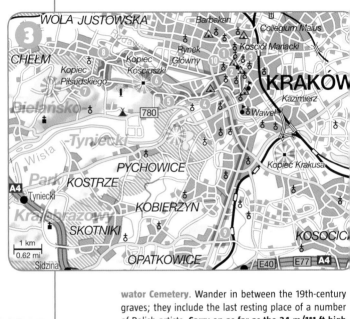

⑥ Kościuszko Mound

wator Cemetery. Wander in between the 19th-century graves; they include the last resting place of a number of Polish artists. **Carry on as far as the 34-m/111-ft-high ⑥ Kościuszko Mound → p. 24** which boasts a unique view of the city. Stop for lunch at the café & restaurant **Kawiarnia pod Kopcem** (Mon–Fri 9am–7pm, Sat/Sun 11am–8pm | Aleja Waszyngtona | tel. 126 62 20 29 | Moderate) in the renovated section of the fortified complex.

⑦ Zoo

⑧ Decius Villa

02:00pm The Aleja Waszyngtona takes you deeper into the **Las Wolski (Wolski Forest)**. At over 1000 acres, it's the largest forest park in Poland. **A quarter of an hour later you reach the ⑦ zoo → p. 95** – get ready to meet the colonies of hippopotamus, mouflon and tapir. **Afterwards, a further 15 minutes' cycling takes you to the ⑧ Decius Villa** in its delightful landscaped garden. **Following Ulica Królowej Jadwigi, Mydlnicka and the Aleja 3 Maja, your route takes you past the National Museum → p. 47 and back to Ulica sw. Anny,** where you can return your bicycle.

⑨ Farmona
Wellness & Spa

⑩ Piec Art

06:00pm By now, you have well and truly earned a bit of pampering: **take a taxi** i to **⑨ Farmona Wellness & Spa → p. 71** and relax with a soothing massage. The day ends with an evening at **⑩ Piec Art → p. 71** over a delicious meal, good cocktails and, if you're lucky, a jazz concert.

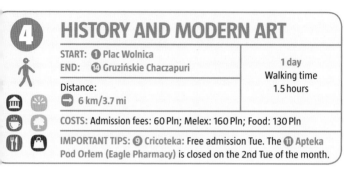

4 HISTORY AND MODERN ART

START: ❶ Plac Wolnica
END: ⓮ Gruzińskie Chaczapuri

Distance:
🚐 6 km/3.7 mi

1 day
Walking time
1.5 hours

COSTS: Admission fees: 60 Pln; Melex: 160 Pln; Food: 130 Pln

IMPORTANT TIPS: ❾ Cricoteka: Free admission Tue. The ⓫ Apteka Pod Orłem (Eagle Pharmacy) is closed on the 2nd Tue of the month.

This walk takes you to the southern side of the Vistula through the suburb of Podgórze, which has enjoyed a real boom in recent years.

09:00am You start your tour on the right bank of the Vistula at ❶ **Plac Wolnica** in Kazimierz. The square was originally only 5 m/15 ft shorter than Krakow's gigantic Market Square. Take time for a hearty breakfast at **Café Młynek** → p. 18 and, suitably fortified, continue towards **the left-hand side of the square.** This is the site of the former Kazimierz Town Hall, which now houses the interesting ❷ **Ethnographic Museum** *(Tue–Sat 10am–7pm | admission 13 Pln | Plac Wolnica 7)*. Admire the two floors of Polish folk art, traditional costumes and furniture. **After that, follow Ulica Bocheńska and turn into Ulica Mostowa** for a stopover at ❸ **Mostowa Art Café** *(Ulica Mostowa 12)* to try some local specialities.

At the end of the street you can already make out the relatively new pedestrian bridge across the Vistula, the ❹ **Kładka Bernatka. Once on the other side, walk down Ulica Brodzińskiego and Staromostowa,** where one of the unconventional ice-cream flavours at ❺ **Lody Si Gela** → p. 55 will sweeten the next stage of the walk. The largest church in the district, ❻ **Kościół św. Józefa (Church of St Joseph)** *(Ulica Zamojskiego 2 | jozef.diecezja.pl)*, stands on **Rynek Podgórski.** Situated directly behind the church, ❼ **Bednarskiego Park** is the perfect place for a break after you look at the church and **before you head off to Ulica Limanowskiego.** The area you are now standing in used to be the ghetto in which Krakow's Jewish population was interned from March 1941 to March 1943. **Make a detour into Ulica Węgierska** to see the remains of the ❽ **Synagoga Zuckera** which was destroyed in the Second World

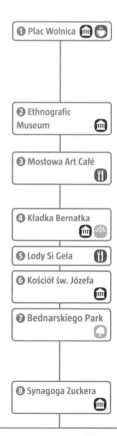

❶ Plac Wolnica 🏛 ☕

❷ Ethnografic Museum 🏛

❸ Mostowa Art Café 🍴

❹ Kładka Bernatka 🏛 🌳

❺ Lody Si Gela 🍴

❻ Kościół św. Józefa 🏛

❼ Bednarskiego Park 🌳

❽ Synagoga Zuckera 🏛

War. Today, the Galerie Starmach *(Mon–Fri 11am–6pm | Ulica Węgierska 5 | www.starmach.com.pl)* for contemporary Polish art is located behind the surviving façade.

01:00pm **If you follow Ulica Limanowskiego, Węgierska and Józefinska** you'll come to the fabulous, ultra-modern art centre, the ⑨ Cricoteka → p. 45, which will introduce you to the work of theatre director, painter and happening artist Tadeusz Kantor and give you INSIDERTIP a great view over the Vistula and Kazimierz. Having left the museum, **turn left and follow Ulica Nadwiślańska as far as Solna. On your right is** ⑩ Plac Bohaterów Getta (Ghetto Heroes Square) → p. 49. The museum at the ⑪ Apteka Pod Orłem (Eagle Pharmacy) → p. 49 commemorates the area's devastating history. **Beyond the railway lines** are the buildings of the former ⑫ Schindler Factory → p. 46, the German Enamelware Factory (DEF). Here, the Museum of the City of Krakow presents its remarkable, 'Krakow under Nazi Occupation 1939–1945' exhibition. Pho-

⑨ Cricoteka

⑩ Plac Bohaterów Getta

⑪ Apteka Pod Orłem

⑫ Schindler Factory

Impressive reminder of Nazi crimes: Ghetto memorial on Plac Bohaterów

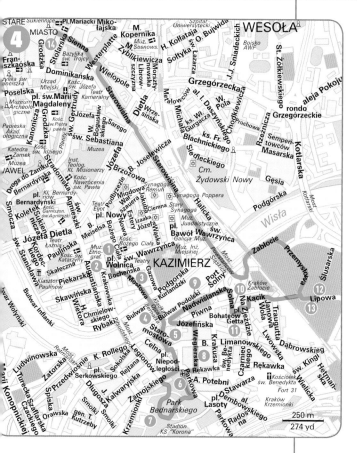

tographs taken during the making of the film 'Schindler's List' hang in the museum café.

05:00pm A combination of art and craftsmanship now awaits you at the 13 Glass and Ceramics Centre *(Mon–Fri 9am–5pm | admission 14 Pln | Ulica Lipowa 3 | www. lipowa3.pl)*. Here you'll watch glass-blowers at work and have the chance to INSIDERTIP buy some unusual souvenirs. Take a ride back to the city centre using a Melex, i.e. one of the **small golf carts parked outside.** Finally, bring your day to a close with some Georgian cooking at ⑭ **Gruzińskie Chaczapuri** *(daily from 12pm | Ulica Sienna 4 | tel. 1 24 29 11 66 | chaczapuri.pl)*.

⑬ Glass and Ceramics Centre

⑭ Gruzińskie Chaczapuri

TRAVEL WITH KIDS

The Poles love children and are fairly open towards having them. Over the past years, Poland has seen a real boom in the number of births. While baby's changing tables, high chairs and play areas are rare to find in restaurants, these services are common available in Krakow's large shopping centres. Nonetheless, the children's activities available to visitors are also rather limited in Krakow. It's, therefore, up to the parents once to show their children just how fascinating the Old Town, the Dragon's Cave and majestic castle really are.

AQUAPARK ● (U D2) (*Ø O*)
This is Poland's largest indoor aqua park, boasting swimming pools that cover over half an acre in size. The main attraction is the 200-m/656-ft-long water slide. For the parents, there's also plenty of things offered in the spa, including yoga and t'ai-chi courses. Adults may also choose to tone up in the fitness rooms or relax in the sauna. You'll also find a restaurant, café and several small shops. *Daily 8am–10pm | admission per hour from 26 Pln, happy hour 8–9am: children 14 Pln, adults 16 Pln, family ticket (3 pers.) 60 Pln/hr | Ulica Dobrego Pasterza 126 | www.parkwodny.pl*

INSIDER TIP ▶ CIUCIU CUKIER ARTIST
(114 B4) (*Ø D6*)
This may possibly be the smallest candy factory in the world! Production tours are offered during which little confectioners in training can learn how these treats are made and then make their own candy creations! If this doesn't give you enough of a sugar shock, head over to the candy shop to buy some handmade goodies to take home with you. The sweets follow recipes from the 17th and 18th centuries! *Production tours start at 11am and repeat at the top of each hour: 9 Pln for children to attend, carers are free | Ulica Grodzka 38 | ciuciukrakow.pl/en*

MUZEUM PRZYRODNICZE PAN (NATURAL HISTORY MUSEUM)
(114 C5) (*Ø E7*)
Marvel at various snakes, lizards, turtles, and frogs. Observe tropical fish and be dazzled by luminescent creatures from the depths of the ocean. There's even a 30,000-year-old woolly rhinoceros on display which was discovered in the Ukrainian village of Starunia in 1929. *Tue–Fri 9am–3pm, Sat/Sun 10am–6pm | children's admission 16 Pln, adults 20 Pln | Ulica św. Sebastiana 9 | 10-minute walk from the Market Square*

Where the wild dragons live: a little bit of imagination is all that is needed, and then the youngsters will love Krakow, too

OGRÓD ZOOLOGICZNY (ZOOLOGICAL GARDENS) (120 B4) (*m b4*)

Built in 1927 and one of Poland's oldest zoos. More than 1500 animals, including 32 endangered species, live on this 49-acre site. Kids are permitted to feed guinea pigs, rabbits, ponies and small pot-bellied pigs at the petting zoo *(food available on site)*. The zoo is located in the beautiful Wolski Forest, making it worth the trip. In May, the azaleas and rhododendrons are in full bloom.

During the week, you can park your car directly at the gate *(parking fee 15 Pln)*. At weekends, however, you have to park half a mile away and take a shuttle bus to the zoo. *Daily 9am–7.30pm | children's admission 10 Pln, adults 18 Pln | Ulica Kasy Oszczędności Miasta Krakowa 14 | zoo-krakow.pl | bus 134 Hotel Cracovia*

INSIDER TIP PARK JORDANA
(112 A6) (*m A6*)

This 49-acre park has footpaths, children's playgrounds, football and vol-leyball pitches, as well as a small lake where kids can have fun in pedalos. Built in 1889, it's Poland's oldest park and was made as a place for children and adolescents to play and do sport. The city's largest meadow, the *Błonia*, is across the street and is a great place for children to romp around. *Ulica Ingardena | tram 15, 18 Park Jordana*

POLONIA WAX MUSEUM
(114 B3) (*m D4*)

Most kids know Scrat, the acorn-driven, sabre-toothed squirrel from 'Ice Age'. But do they know he's roommates with Spiderman and Joker? Maybe not. How's it even possible for these personalities to live together? Well, this wax museum has worked wonders! The kids may not enjoy seeing John Paul II and the other Polish celebrities, but what about Harry and Hermione? *Daily 9.30–10pm | admission 30 Pln, ask about discount rates at the counter | Rynek Główny 34 | www.poloniawaxmuseum.com*

FESTIVALS & EVENTS

People in Krakow like to celebrate and do so whenever they can – usually on the Rynek Główny, but during the City Festival in June all of Krakow becomes a gigantic stage. There are many other open-air festivals in the calendar, along with concerts and processions through the streets. Information under *www.biurofestiwalowe.pl* or from the tourist information office.

MARCH/APRIL

The *Dni Bachowskie (Bach Days)* at the end of the month are organised by the Krakow Music Academy. Lectures and performances of Baroque music (not only by Bach) played by Krakow students and other musicians. *www.amuz.krakow.pl*

One-week *Misteria Paschalia* festival with classical concerts in churches, the Philharmonic Hall and the opera house. Theme: Lent and Easter. *www.misteriapaschalia.pl.*

Starzy i Mlodzi czyli Jazz w Krakowie (Old and New – Jazz in Krakow): famous and not-so-famous musicians give concerts in jazz cellars, clubs and cafés. *www.krakow-jazz.pl*

MAY

You will be able to visit most of the collections almost free of charge on the *Noc Muzeów w Krakowie (Long Night of the Museums)*. A specially-minted 1 Pln coin is your admission ticket. This event is extremely popular and you should thus expect long queues at the various museums.

JUNE

Concerts, parades, marathon runs are all part of the *Święto Miasta (City Festival)* at the beginning of June. The highlight is the ● *Parada Smoków (Dragon Parade)* when those taking part pull gigantic colourful dragons through Krakow's streets.

The *Wianki (Vistula Wreath Festival)* at midsummer brings back memories of pagan days when young girls cast wreaths into the water on the longest night of the year in the hope that fate would send them a loving husband. Also on the programme concerts by familiar and unknown Polish bands and a firework display.

Kazimierz celebrates the ★ *Festiwal Kultury Żydowskiej (Festival of Jewish Culture)* with concerts, films and exhibitions. Also fascinating guided tours to

Krakow bubbles with joie de vivre, and it is not only during the Festival of Jewish Culture that it enjoys exuberant celebrations

places that are otherwise closed *www. jewishfestival.pl*

AUGUST

The *Targi Sztuki Ludowej (Folk Art Markets)* focuses on the arts and crafts of Krakow. Traditional products made of wood and clay are sold on the Rynek Główny.

SEPTEMBER

On the 1st Sunday of the month, you'll witness thousands of dog owners showing off their costumed darlings at the *Marsz Jamników (Dachshund Parade)* The INSIDER TIP *Festiwal Sacrum Profanum* is a week-long music festival held in unusual locations. Some examples include the former Schindler Factory and the rolling mill in Nowa Huta. You'll hear all music genres of 20th-century music ranging from jazz to electronic music. There's also classical music, ballet and jazz at the Philharmonic Hall. *www. sacrumprofanum.pl*

DECEMBER

From the 2nd Satuarday of the month, the *Targi Bożonarodzeniowe (Christmas Market)* takes over the Market Square. The most beautiful nativity cribs are chosen at the INSIDER TIP *Konkurs Szopek Krakowskich (Christmas Crèche Contest)* on the Market Square. These are then exhibited in the Historical Museum. *Muzeum Historyczne Miasta Krakowa (Ulica Lubicz 16 | mhk.pl)*

PUBLIC HOLIDAYS

1 Jan	New Year
March/April	Easter Monday
1 May	Labour Day
3 May	Constitution Day
May/June	Corpus Christi
15 Aug	Assumption
1 Nov	All Saints' Day
11 Nov	Independence Day
25/26 Dec	Christmas

LINKS, BLOGS, APPS & MORE

LINKS & BLOGS

karnet.krakow.pl/en Listings magazine showcasing Krakow's varied cultural and entertainment programme, from music, literature, theatre and exhibitions to cinema and the various festivals

en.poland.gov.pl This official promotional website provides loads of useful and interesting information about Poland in general. The site is well structured and topics range from history, geography and culture to science, business and politics

www.local-life.com/Krakow As the name suggests, a forum with a lively, well-informed English-language guide, covering all aspects of life in Krakow

krakow4u.pl/eng_index.php?parametr= eng_glowna_s Dozens of fabulous photos of Krakow; the 360° shots of the sights are particularly impressive

www.fleetinglife.com/2014/08/09/ things-to-do-in-krakow-jazz-scene For those who didn't know that Krakow was a global jazz hub – a homage to the city's jazz tradition

krakow.travel/en Attractive official city travel guide produced by the Krakow Festival Office

en.biurofestiwalowe.pl The website of the Krakow Festival Office has in-depth information on a host of internationally acclaimed cultural events taking place in the city

www.urbantravelblog.com/guide/kra kow Professional travel writers offer their take on Krakow, communicating the spirit of the city and the people.

krakowski.blox.pl/html The texts in the 'Krakow Day by Day' photo-blog are unfortunately not available in English, but the great pictures speak for themselves

Regardless of whether you are still researching your trip or already in Krakow: these addresses will provide you with more information, videos and networks to make your holiday even more enjoyable

www.spottedbylocals.com/krakow What do the locals recommend when they receive guests in their home town?

www.polishpod101.com & bloggypolish.co.uk Two 'slightly' different approaches to learning Polish with podcasts!

www.couchsurfing.org Krakow also has quite a number of followers in the worldwide network of couchsurfers. Around 34,500 Krakow inhabitants offer travellers their couch, their hospitality and their local knowledge

VIDEOS & MUSIC

www.youtube.com/watch?v=QKs1n_iIFe8 Video with impressions of a trip with the water tram down the Vistula. Polish commentary with English subtitles

http://worldcam.eu/webcams/poland/krakow Collection of webcams scattered throughout the city with views of the Wawel, Rynek Główny, the university and other places

www.youtube.com/watch?v=Xmg-7R72caQ&feature=related You can experience the abbreviated rendition of the *Hejnał* live from the tower of St Mary's Church

www.youtube.com/watch?v=Cr4YE_hh4HI The finale of the Krakow Festival of Jewish Culture is a uniquely exhilarating klezmer concert

short.travel/kra14 A beautifully made, two-part documentary on the Krakow district of Podgórze

APPS

Krakow in my pocket Useful app when working out how to get from A to B

Around me This app for iPhone and Android searches the area you're in to provide your a list of nearby hotels, ATMs, restaurants, pubs etc.

TRAVEL TIPS

ARRIVAL

✈ All national and international flights land at *Kraków Airport (www.krakowairport.pl)*. There are regular services from the UK operated by the Polish airline LOT *(www.lot.com)*, British Airways *(www.britishairways.com)* EasyJet *(www.easyjet.com)* and Ryanair *(www.ryanair.com)*. You can take bus 292 or 208 from the airport – both travel to the main train station (3.80 Pln) – or the train that takes you there directly. There is a shuttle bus from the airport (200 m/220 yd away) to the station; the ticket costs 4 Pln. The train departs every 30 minutes and the trip to the main station takes 16 minutes. A taxi to the centre of Krakow costs around 40 Pln.

🚗 It is about 1430 km/890 mi from London to Krakow in a straight line (which would be straight across Belgium, Germany and south-east from Wrocław).

RESPONSIBLE TRAVEL

It doesn't take a lot to be environmentally friendly whilst travelling. Don't just think about your carbon footprint whilst flying to and from your holiday destination but also about how you can protect nature and culture abroad. As a tourist it is especially important to respect nature, look out for local products, cycle instead of driving, save water and much more. If you would like to find out more about eco-tourism please visit: *www.ecotourism.org*

Not exactly to be recommended for a weekend trip!

🚆 The train is no problem. Take the lunchtime Eurostar to Brussels, the high-speed train to Cologne and then the overnight sleeper train 'Jan Kiepura' from Cologne to Warsaw. There are direct connections from Warsaw to Krakow. Alternatively, take the Eurostar to Paris and then the City Night Line sleeper from Paris to Berlin and an express train to Warsaw. Travelling across Europe is great fun. For train information, see *www.seat61.com*

BANKS & EXCHANGE

There are not only branches of all major banks in Krakow *(in general: Mon–Fri 7.30am–5pm, Sat 7.30am–2pm)* but also privately operated exchange offices: *kantor (daily 9am–7pm)*. However, it is much less complicated to take money from one of the many cash dispensers in the city using your EC or credit card.

CONSULATES & EMBASSIES

BRITISH EMBASSY
Ulica Kawalerii 12 | 00-468 Warsaw | tel. +48 22 311 00 00 | ukinpoland.fco.gov.uk/en/

U.S. CONSULATE GENERAL
Ulica Stolarska 9 | 31-043 Krakow | tel. +48 124 24 51 00 | poland.usembassy.gov

CANADIAN EMBASSY
Ulica Jana Matejki 1/5 | 00-481 Warsaw | tel. +48 22 584 31 00 | www.canadainternational.gc.ca/poland-pologne

From arrival to weather

Your holiday from start to finish: the most important addresses and information for your Krakow trip

CURRENCY

Poland's national currency is the *złoty* (Pln) (1 *złoty* = 100 *groszy*). It is sometimes possible to pay in euros; only notes are accepted and the change is given in *złoty*.

CUSTOMS

Goods for personal consumption can be imported and exported tax-free in the EU including 800 cigarettes, 10 litres of spirits, 90 litres of wine and 110 litres of beer. It is necessary to get authorisation from the Polish Ministry of Culture if you wish to export any antiques made before 9 May 1945.

Travellers to the United States who are returning residents of the country do not have to pay duty on articles purchased overseas up to the value of $800, but there are limits on the amount of alcoholic beverages and tobacco products. For the regulations for international travel for U.S. residents please see *www.cbp.gov*

CYCLING

All in all, there are only around 30 km/19 mi of marked cycle lanes in Krakow, but at least it's nice and flat! The prettiest and safest places to ride are along the Vistula (to Tyniec or Nowa Huta), in Błonia, the Planty and in Las Wolski (Wolski Forest). This area has a lot of steep inclines, so mountain bikes and e-bikes are also available. The average price to rent a bike is 50 to 60 Pln/day. E-bikes are 100 Pln/day.

Bike hire: the most central is *Krk Bike Rental* (114 B3) (*ψ D5*) (daily 9am to sundown | Ulica św. Anny 4 | www.bike-rental.pl). Mountain bikes and e-bikes are also offered for those looking to do a sporting tour. In Kazimierz, you'll find *Dwa koła* (118 B4) (*ψ E8*) (Mon–Fri 9am–5pm, Sat 10am–2pm | Ulica Józefa 5 | www.dwakola.internetdsl.pl). We also recommend *Art-Bike* (118 B1) (*ψ F7*) (Mon–Fri 10am–6pm, Sat 10am–2pm | Ulica Starowiślna 33a).

DRIVING

The speed limit on motorways is 140 km/h (85 mph); in built-up areas (white signs) and within towns (green signs) 50 km/h – 60 km/h (30 mph – 35 mph) from 11pm to 6am. There are frequent speed checks! Dipped beams are obligatory during the day and there must be a reflective vest in the boot.

If you do decide to drive to Krakow, you will soon discover that parking in the city is anything but easy. The inner city is divided into three parking zones: Zone A (centre) is reserved for pedestrians. You are only allowed to drive to your hotel to unload your luggage; parking is strictly prohibited. There is a speed limit of 20 km/h (12 mph) in Zone B and you are only permitted to park at a limited number of marked spaces. Parking is permitted in Zone C after you have paid the appropriate fee: 3 Pln for the first hour on weekdays between 10am and 6pm (free at weekends). You can buy parking tickets from machines (only cash and the machines don't give change). The minimum fee is 1 Pln/20 min. Ideally, ask about parking facilities when you book your hotel.

ELECTRICITY

220 volt alternating current with the (type C & E) Europlug.

EMERGENCY SERVICES

Police *tel. 997*; fire brigade *tel. 998*, ambulance *tel. 999*

IMMIGRATION

Citizens of the U.K. & Ireland, U.S., Canada, Australia and New Zealand need only a valid passport to enter all countries of the EU. Children below the age of 12 need a children's passport.

INFORMATION ABROAD

POLISH NATIONAL TOURISM OFFICE
UK: 10 Heathfield Terrace | London W4 4JE | tel. +44 774 770 180 6 or +44 208 991 707 6 | www.poland.travel/en-gb

USA: 5 Marine View Plaza, Suite 303b | Hoboken, NJ 07030-5722 | tel. +1 201 420 99 10 | www.poland.travel/en-us

TOURIST INFORMATION

They're hard to tell apart, but there are many public *(informacja)* and private information offices in the centre of Krakow. The private ones also offer tours for you to book, including excursions to Zakopane, Wieliczka, Auschwitz and other destinations. The *Karnet Magazin*, a brochure listing all the current events in Polish and English that is published monthly, is available at *Ulica Jana 2* (114 B3) *(⑪ D4)*. Additional information offices: *Informacja Wieża Ratuszowa* (114 B3) *(⑪ D5) (Rynek Główny 1 | Town Hall Tower)*; *Tourist Information MCIT (Małopolskie Centrum Informacji Turystycznej)* (114 B3) *(⑪ D5) (Rynek Główny 1/3 | Cloth Hall | infokrakow.pl)*

INTERNET & WI-FI

There are two wi-fi zones in Krakow: on the Market Square *(net name: Krakow123)* and on Ulica Szeroka in Kazimierz, and both have a sluggish connection. Many cafés and most restaurants provide somewhat faster Internet access.

FOR BOOKWORMS AND FILM BUFFS

Unseen Hand – Adam Zagajewski, one of the world's master poets has written a brilliant new collection of prose in which he returns to themes that have played an important role in his career – meditations on language, place, and history (2011)

The Girl in the Red Coat – As a child, Roma Ligocka survived the Holocaust in the Krakow ghetto (2003)

Schindler's List – Shot in Krakow, Steven Spielberg's film recounts the story of the 1100 Jews saved by Oskar Schindler (1993)

The Cracow Ghetto Pharmacy – Tadeusz Pankiewicz was the only non-Jew allowed to stay in the Krakow ghetto and run the pharmacy. His memoir reports on the horrific cruelty that he witnessed while he was there (1982)

A password, which you will be given free of charge by the waiter or waitress (for a limited period), is usually necessary. Internet cafés are uncommon in Krakow.

MEDICAL SERVICES

The same conditions apply as for all other EU countries. The European Insurance Card guarantees treatment for those legally insured; the costs are refunded in keeping with the rates in your home country (don't forget the bills!). Travel insurance is necessary for any additional services.

OPENING HOURS

Poland introduced a new trade law in 2018 which changed and restricted the opening hours for stores on Sunday. And in 2020, many businesses won't be able to open at all on Sunday. These laws won't apply to every business (e.g. bakeries or petrol stations) and even the shopping centres, larger shops, and supermarkets will be able to open on the last Sunday of the month. It's still not certain how this will all be enforced, but, until this decision is made, Poland's retailers are working to find a way around these restrictions.

During the week, most shops open from 10am to 6pm and on Saturday, they close at 3pm. There are food shops in the centre of town that stay open until 10pm or even around the clock. The large shopping centres and chain stores are open until 10pm during the week and 8pm on Saturday.

PERSONAL SAFETY

Krakow is one of the safest towns in Poland; normal precautions are sufficient. Watch out for pickpocketers in large crowds of people. There are usually no problems in the inner city at night but you should avoid districts such as Nova Huta and Podgórze when it is dark.

PHONE & MOBILE PHONE

Dialling code for Australia: *0061*, Canada: *001*, Ireland: *00353*, UK: *0044*, USA: *001*. Dialling code for Poland: *0048*. then the complete number, without the zero before the area code. For connections from mobile to mobile, however, always dial the zero.

BUDGETING

Beer	from £2/$3.10 *for 0.5 litres in a restaurant*
Cappuccino	from £1.60/$2.50 *for a cup in a café*
Pizza	from £5/$8 *in a restaurant*
Club	from £5/$6 *per person*
Museum	from £1/$1.60 *per person*
Bus	from £0.50/$0.70 *for one trip*

Although roaming charges have been abolished in the EU, it may be cheaper to make calls using a Polish prepaid SIM (e.g. a 'karta SIM' at the post office). SIM cards must be registered in person, so buying one can take a bit of time.

POST

You can purchase stamps and envelopes from the post office (poczta). The most central ones are the *post office on Plac Wszystkich Świętych 9* (114 B4) (*∅ D5*) *(Mon–Fri 8am–6pm)* and the *main post* office (114 C4) (📍 E5) (Mon–Fri 8am–8.30pm, Sat 8am–3pm | Ulica Westerplatte 20), the post office at Ulica Lubicz 4 (115 D2) (📍 E–F 3–4) (near the train station) is open 24 hours a day. Postcards and letters up to 50 g: 6 Pln to all European destinations.

PUBLIC TRANSPORT

You'll spend most of your time on foot in Krakow. If you want to visit the outskirts, then it's fastest and cheapest to travel by bus or tram; most run until around 11pm. A ticket (billet autobusowy) costs 3.80 Pln. You can buy tickets from machines and some trafik, kiosks that sell newspapers, cigarettes and drinks. There are two ticket booths in the centre: Ulica Podwale 3/5 (114 A3) (📍 C4) and Ulica Mogilska 15a (U C3) (📍 J3) (both Mon–Fri 7am–7pm). A ticket is valid for one journey; you have

to buy another one if you change. In such cases, it is better to buy a one-hour ticket that includes changes (5 Pln). Also available: 24, 48 and 72-hour tickets (15 Pln, 24 Pln and 36 Pln) or a week's pass (48 Pln).

SIGHTSEEING & GUIDED TOURS

Melek is a transportation service that allows you to tour the city on a golf cart via fixed routes (from 40 Pln).
How much you pay with Cracow Free Walkative Tours (www.freewalkingtour.com) is entirely up to you. There's a two-hour tour through the Old Town from Fri–Sun, for example, which starts every day at 10am at the Krakow Barbican. This one is paid for via donation, as is the afternoon excursion to Kazimierz (2pm). The downside is being part of a large group.

WEATHER IN KRAKOW

	Jan	Feb	March	April	May	June	July	Aug	Sept	Oct	Nov	Dec
Daytime temperatures in °C/°F	–1/30	2/36	7/45	14/57	19/66	22/72	24/75	24/75	20/68	13/55	7/45	2/36
Nighttime temperatures in °C/°F	–6/21	–5/23	–1/30	4/39	9/48	12/54	15/59	14/57	10/50	5/41	1/34	–3/27
☀	1	2	3	5	6	7	7	6	5	3	2	1
☂	8	7	8	8	11	12	10	9	8	8	9	10

Take a hop-on/hop-off bus tour with *Wow Krakow! (daily 9.30am-6pm | wowkrakow. pl)* and take in the city from a red convertible bus. Tickets are available online, on the bus or at several points of sale. They are valid for one or two days (60 or 90 Pln). The ticket allows you to get on and off as often as you'd like. A single tour (40 Pln) is also available.

The *Communism Tour (2.5 hours | 159 Pln/ person)* of Nowa Huta by the *Crazy Guides (www.crazyguides.com)* invokes the history of the district between 1945 and 1989. Their most popular tour includes lunch and a visit to an apartment furnished in the style of the time. It lasts four hours and costs 170 Pln per person.

The ride in a *horse-drawn carriage (30 min. from Market Square to the Wawel | 150 Pln)* for 4–5 passengers also stops at the main square. Officially, only licensed guides are allowed to give city tours of Krakow. Book through the *Marco der Pole travel agency (krakow-travel. com)*. Joanna Tumielewicz, the author of this guide, also shows visitors round the city *(tumielewiczj@interia.pl)*.

From April to October, you can discover the city from the river, on board the 'Nimfa' and the 'Orka', two ships used for the ● *Vistula tours (117 D4) (ꙮ C8) (Bulwar Czerwieński 3 | dock Przystań Wawel, in front of Grunwaldzki Bridge | mob. 5 30 75 07 36 | www.statekkrakow.com)*. The one-hour cruises start between 9am and 6pm and cost 30 Pln. The three-hour trip on Sunday (65 Pln) with the 'Nimfa' leaves at 4pm (May–Oct daily) and is combined with a one-hour stop to visit the Benedictine abbey in Tyniec.

Cracow City Tours (tel. 124 211333 | www.cracowcitytours.com) offers tours to Auschwitz *(155 Pln | Start: Plac Matejki 2)*. The total travel time takes about three hours, and you'll need another three hours to tour the site.

CURRENCY CONVERTER

£	PLN	PLN	£
1	5.20	1	0.20
3	15.50	3	0.60
5	26	5	1
13	67	13	2.50
40	207	40	7.70
75	388	75	14.50
120	620	120	23
250	1295	250	48
500	2590	500	97

$	PLN	PLN	$
1	3.30	1	0.30
3	10	3	0.90
5	16.50	5	1.50
13	43	13	4
40	132	40	12
75	247	75	23
120	395	120	36
250	825	250	75
500	1650	500	150

For current exchange rates see www.xe.com

TAXIS

Taxis are relatively inexpensive. There are several taxi ranks in the centre, and elsewhere you can use your mobile phone to call one. Normally, the taximeter is turned on: it usually shows 5 Pln when you get in and then there is a kilometre charge starting at 3 Pln depending on the tariff (weekday, holiday, day/night rate). *Radio taxis e. g. Mega Taxi (the cheapest option, tel. 196 25) or Barbakar (tel. 196 61)*

TIPPING

Tips are not included in the total price, and it is customary to round up the bill. In higher-class restaurants, a 10 per cent tip is usually given.

USEFUL PHRASES POLISH

PRONUNCIATION

In Polish, sentences are often formed depending on the gender of the speaker or the person being addressed. That is why, in some cases, there are two versions in this list of phrases: the first is masculine; the second, feminine.

IN BRIEF

Yes/No/Maybe	tak [tuk]/nie [nyay]/może [moshay]
Please/Thank you	Proszę [Proshen]/Dziękuję [Djenkooyay]
Excuse me, please	Przepraszam! [Psheprashamm]
May I ...?	Czy mogę ...? [Tschi moshay ...?]
Pardon?	Słucham? [Suukamm?]
I would like to .../	Chciałbym/Chciałabym ... [Chowbim/-chowabim ...]/
Have you got ...?	Czy ma pan/pani ...? [Chi ma pan/pani ...?]
How much is ...	Ile to kosztuje ...? [Iletta kostooya ...?]
I (don't) like that	To mi się (nie) podoba
	[To mi shen (nyay) podobba]
good/bad	dobrze/źle [dobshey/shlay]
broken/doesn't work	rozbity/nie działa [rosbyeti/nyay tsiaua]
too much/much/little	za dużo/dużo/mało [za dusho/duscho/maavo]
all/nothing	wszystko/nic [shistko/neets]
Help!/Attention!/	Ratunku!/Uwaga!/Ostrożnie!
Caution!	[Ratunnku!/Uvaga!/Ostroshniyeh!]
ambulance	karetka pogotowia [karetka pogotoviya]
police/fire brigade	policja/straż pożarna [policia/strash posharna]
danger/dangerous	niebezpieczeństwo/niebezpieczny
	[nyebyestpetshtvo/nyebyestpetshnya]

GREETINGS, FAREWELL

Good morning!/afternoon!	Dzień dobry! [jen dobry!]
Good evening!/night!	Dobry wieczór!/Dobranoc!
	[Dobbri vechor!/Dobbranots!]
Hello!/Goodbye!	Witam!/Do widzenia! [Vitam!/Do vidseniya!]
See you!	Cześć! [Chesh!]
My name is ...	Nazywam się ... [Nasivam shen ...]
What's your name?	Jak się nazywasz? [Yak shen nasivash?]
I'm from ...	Pochodzę z ... [Pokodsen s ...]

Czy mówisz po polsku?

'Do you speak Polish?' This guide will help you to say the basic words and phrases in Polish

DATE & TIME

Monday/Tuesday	poniedziałek/wtorek [ponyedsyavek/vstorrek]
Wednesday/Thursday	środa/czwartek [srodda/chvartekk]
Friday/Saturday	piątek/sobota [piyontekk/sobotta]
Sunday	niedziela [nyedsyella]
working day	dzień roboczy [jen robottchi]
holiday	dzień świąteczny [jen sviyontetshni]
today/tomorrow/	dziś/jutro [dyish/yutro]/
yesterday	wczoraj [vchorai]
hour/minute	godzina/minuta [godsina/minuta]
day/night/week	dzień/noc/tydzień [jen/notts/tidshinya]
What time is it?	Która godzina? [Ktura godsina?]

TRAVEL

open/closed	otwarte/zamknięte [otvarteh/samkniyente]
entrance/vehicle entrance	wejście/wyjście [veyshyeh/veeshyeh]
departure/arrival	odjazd/przyjazd [odyast/pshiyast]
toilets – ladies/	toaleta damska [toaletta damska]/
toilets – gentlemen	toaleta męska [myanska]
(no) drinking water	Woda nie zdatna do picia/Woda pitna [Voda statna do pidya/Voda pitna]
Where is ...?/	Gdzie jest ...? [Gsay yest...?]
Where are ...?	Gdzie są ...? [Gsay song ...?]
left/right	na lewo/na prawo [na levo/na prahvo]
straight ahead/back	prosto/spowrotem [prosto/spavrottem]
close/far	blisko/daleko [blisko/dalehko]
bus/tram	autobus/tramwaj [autobus/tramveye]
metro/taxi	metro/taxi [metro/taxi]
street map/map	mapa miasta/mapa [mapa myasta/mapa]
train station	dworzec/lotnisko [dvashek/lotnissko]
schedule/ticket	rozkład jazdy/bilet [roskvad yasdeh/bilyet]
train/track	pociąg/tor [posiyong/tor]
platform	peron [peron]
I would like to rent ...	Chciałbym/Chciałabym wynająć ... [Chaubim/Chauabim vinayonts ...]
a car/a bicycle	samochód/rower [sammachod/rover]
petrol/gas station	stacja benzynowa [statsya bensinova]
petrol (gas)/diesel	benzyna/ropy [bensina/roppi]
breakdown/	awaria [avahrya]/
repair shop	warsztat [varshtatt]

FOOD & DRINK

Could you please book a table for tonight for four?	Proszę zarezerwować dla nas na dziś wieczór jeden stolik dla czterech osób [Proshen sareservovatsch dla nas na dsish vechor stollik na tchteri ossobbi]
The menu, please	Czy mogę prosić kartę? [tchi moschay prossits kartenn?]
Could I please have ...?	Chciałbym/chciałabym ...? [Chaubim/chauabim?]
vegetarian/ allergy	wegetarianin/wegetarianka [vegetarianin/ vegetariyanka]/alergia [allergiya]
May I have the bill, please	Proszę o rachunek! [Proshen o rachunek!]

SHOPPING

Where can I find ...?	Przepraszam, gdzie jest ...? [Psheprasham, gsay yest,...?]
I'd like .../ I'm looking for ...	Chciałbym/Chciałabym ... [Chaubim/Chauabim ...]
pharmacy/chemist	apteka/drogeria [aptyeka/drogeriya]
shopping centre	centrum handlowe [sentrum handloveh]
kiosk	kiosk [kiosk]
expensive/cheap/price	drogo/tanio/cena [droga/tannio/tsyena]
more/less	więcej/mniej [viyensay/mniniyey]
organically grown	produkt ekologiczny [pradukt ekologitchni]

ACCOMMODATION

I have booked a room	Zarezerwowałem/zarezerwowałam pokój [Sareservovavmem/Saraservovavam pokui]
Do you have any ... left?	Czy ma pan/pani jeszcze ...? [Chi ma pan/panyi yestchey ...?]
single room	pokój jednoosobowy [pockui yednossobovi]
double room	pokój dwuosobowy [pockui dvosobbovi]
breakfast/ half board	ze śniadaniem/ze śniadaniem i kolacją [se shnyadanyam /se shnyadanyam i kollatsiya]
full board (American plan)	z pełnym wyżywieniem [s poynim visiviyeniem]
at the front	od frontu [odd frontu]
shower/sit-down bath	prysznic/łazienka [prichnyits/wasyenka]
balcony/terrace	balkon/taras [balkon/taras]
key/room card	klucz/karta [klootch/karta]
luggage/suitcase/bag	bagaż/walizka/torba [bagasch/valiska/torba]

BANKS, MONEY & CREDIT CARDS

bank/ATM	bank/bankomat [bank/bankomat]
pin code	kod PIN [kod PIN]

I'd like to change ...	Chciałbym/Chciałabym wymienić ... [Chaubim/Chauabim vimenyitch ...]
cash/credit card	gotówka/karta kredytowa [gatuvka/karta kreditova]
bill/coin	banknot/moneta [banknott/moneta]

HEALTH

doctor/dentist/ paediatrician	lekarz/dentysta/pediatra [läkasch/dentista/pädiatra]
hospital/emergency clinic	szpital/pogotowie [schpital/pogotowwijä]
fever/pain	gorączka/ból [gorontschka/bul]
diarrhoea/nausea	rozwolnienie/nudności [roswolniänä/nudnusjzi]
pain reliever/tablet	środek przeciwbólowy/tabletka [sroddeck pschäziwbulowi/tablättka]

POST, TELECOMMUNICATIONS & MEDIA

stamp/ letter	znaczek pocztowy [snatchek potchtovi]/ list [list]
postcard	pocztówka [potchtoovka]
I need a landline phone card	Potrzebna mi karta telefoniczna do telefonu domowego [Potchebna mi karta telefonitshna do telefonu domovyeygo]
I'm looking for a prepaid card for my mobile	Szukam karty startowej do telefonu komórkowego [shukam karti startovay do telefonu komurkovego]
Where can I find Internet access?	Gdzie znajdę dojście do internetu? [Gsay snidyen doysiya do internetu?]
socket/charger	kontakt/ładowarka [kontakt/wadovarka]
computer/battery	computer/bateria [komputer/bateriya]
Internet connection/ wifi	dojście do internetu [doysiya do internetu]/ bezprzewodowy dostęp do internetu [byespshevodovi dosten do internetu]

NUMBERS

0	zero [sero]	10	dziesięć [dyeshentsh]
1	jeden [yeyden]	11	jedenaście [jedenashtya]
2	dwa [dva]	12	dwanaście [dvanashtya]
3	trzy [tshi]	20	dwadzieścia [dvadshastya]
4	cztery [chteri]	50	pięćdziesiąt [pyendyisont]
5	pięć [pyench]	70	siedemdziesiąt [schedemmdyisont]
6	sześć [shesht]	100	sto [sto]
7	siedem [shedemm]	1000	tysiąc [tishonts]
8	osiem [oshemm]	½	jedna druga [jedna druga]
9	dziewięć [djeventsh]	¼	jedna czwarta [jedna tchvarta]

STREET ATLAS

The green line indicates the Discovery Tour 'Krakow at a glance'
The blue line indicates the other Discovery Tours

All tours are also marked on the pull-out map

Photo: Rynek Główny (Market Place)

Exploring Krakow

The map on the back cover shows how the area has been sub-divided

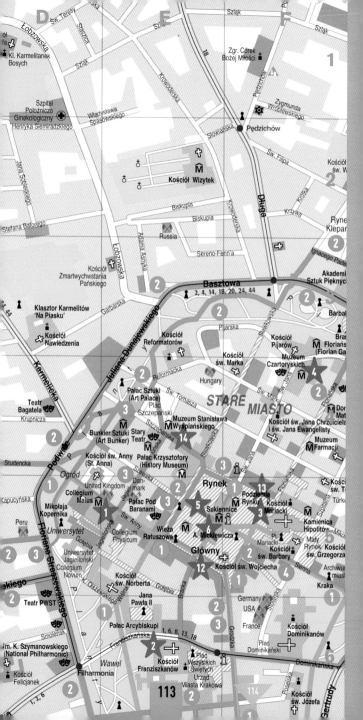

A
B
C

1

2

3

6

Stefana Batorego

Biskupia
Konopnicka
Krzywa

Hynek
Kleparski

Russia

Sereno-Fenn'a

Długa

Ignacego Paderewskiego

Jan

Akademia
Sztuk Pięknych

Grunwaldz

Łobzowska

Adama Asnyka

Kościół
Zmartwychwstania
Pańskiego

Basztowa
2, 4, 14, 18, 20, 24, 44

Barbakan

Klasztor Karmelitów
'Na Piasku'

Garbarska

Pijarska

Kościół
Pijarów

Brama
Floriańska
(Florian Gate)

Barb
Mury Ob
(City Wall)

Kościół
Nawiedzenia

Kościół
Reformatorów

Kościół
św. Marka

Muzeum
Czartoryskich

A. Fred

Karmelicka

Reformacka

Hungary

STARE MIASTO

Dom Jana
Matejki

Teatr
Bagatela

Krupnicza

Pałac Sztuki
(Art Palace)

Plac
Szczepański

Muzeum Stanisława
Wyspiańskiego

Kościół św. Jana Chrzciciela
i św. Jana Ewangelisty

Dom Pod

Bunkier Sztuki
(Art Bunker)

Stary
Teatr

Muzeum
Farmacji

Studencka

Kościół św. Anny
(St. Anna)

Pałac Krzysztofory
(History Museum)

Rynek

Podziemia
Rynku

Kościół
św. Tomasza

Türkel

Kapucyńska

Ogród

United Kingdom

Dan-
mark

Sukiennice

Kościół
Mariacki

Peru

Mikołaja
Kopernika

Collegium
Maius

Pałac Pod
Baranami

Kamienica
Hipolitów

Uniwersytet

Collegium
Physicum

Wieża
Ratuszowa

A. Mickiewicza

Rynek
Główny

Mały
Rynek

Kościół
św. Grzegorza

Uniwersytet
Jagielloński
Collegium
Novum

Kościół
św. Norberta

Jana
Pawła II

Kościół św. Wojciecha

Archiwum
miasta

Kraka

Germany
USA

Na Gr

Teatr PWST

Smoleńsk

France

Kościół
Dominikanów

Pałac Arcybiskupi

1, 6, 8, 13, 18

Plac
Dominikański

Dominikańska

...onia im. K. Szymanowskiego
...ational Philharmonic)

Kościół
Franciszkanów

Plac
Wszystkich
Świętych

Wawel
Filharmonia

Urząd
Miasta Krakowa

Kościół
św. Józefa

Kościół
Felicjanek

Poselska

Muzeum
Archeologiczne

Senacka

św. Gertrudy

NOWY
ŚWIAT

Plac Na

Centrum Kultury Ukraińskiej

Plac Marii
Magdaleny

Kanonicza

Kościół św. Piotra
i Pawła

Pałac Biskupa Erazma Ciołka

Muzeum
Archidiecezjalne

Centrum
Jana Pawła II

Kościół św.
Andrzeja

Kościół
św. Marcina

6, 8, 10, 13, 18

Sw. Gertrudy

Powiśle

Groblach

Podzamcze

Kościół
św. Idziego

Bulwar Czerwieński

Muzeum
Katedralne

Katedra
Wawelska

Zamek

Muzeum
Geologiczne

Wawel

Wawel
Plac
Bernardyński

Kościół
Księży Misjonarzy

STRAD

WISŁA

200 m

219 yd

Kościół
św. Bernardyna

Klasztor i Kościół
Bernardynów

Smocza Jama
(Dragon Cave)

117

114

Kraków Główny

Akademia
Ekonomiczna

Kościół
św. Floriana

Kurniki

Dworzec
Główny
Zachód

Uniwersytet
Ekonomiczny

Aleksandra

Opera Krakowska

Topolowa

Topolowa

Zygmunta Augusta

Kurkowa

Ogród
Strzeleckiego

Zygmunta
Augusta

Jana
Sobieskiego

Radziwiłłowska

4, 10, 14, 20, 44, 52

Lubicz

Plac
Kolejowy

Lubicz

Lubicz

Lubicz

WESOŁA

2, 4, 10, 14, 20, 44, 52

Kościół
Karmelitanek
Bosych

im.
sza Słowackiego
usz Słowacki Theatre)

Szpi

Ludwika Zamenhofa

Strzelecka

Uniwers

ża
oss)

Marii
Skłodowskiej-Curie

Pomnik
I. Łukasiewicza

Bazylika Najświętszego
Serca Pana Jezusa

Mikołaja Kopernika

Kościół Niepokolanego
Poczęcia NP Marii

Colle

Gmach Towarzystwa
Lekarskiego

Państwowy Szpital
Kliniczny

Medicu

3, 10, 24, 52
or

Mikołaja Kopernika

GRZEGÓRZKI

Kościół
św. Mikołaja
(St. Nikolaus)

Błich

Hugona Kołłątaja

Odona

Bujnida

Zespół
Klinik
CMUJ

Mikołaja Zyblikiewicza

Moskorzewskiego

Sołtyka

Jana Andrzeja Snadeckich

Ludwinowska

Bonerowska

Błich

Józefa Dietla

Św. Łazarza

Bo ko VI

Grzegórzecka

Grzegórzecka

1, 12, 19, 22

Józefa Dietla

Wrześniska

Michała Siedleckiego

Al. Ignacego Daszyńskiego

Winterego Pola

Chodowieckiego

Jana Karola Chodowieckiego

Kot

Starowiślna

3, 17, 19, 24

ks. Władysława
Gurgacza

Wygoda

Prochowa

Berka Joselewicza

ks. Franciszka Blachnickiego

Miodowa

Michała Siedleckiego

Św. Sebastiana

Berka Joselewicza

Starowiślna

Miodowa

Miodowa

Nowy Cmentarz Żydowski
(New Jewish Cemetery)

119

Gal
Kazi

Brzozowa

Synagoga
Tempel

Miodowa

Skałeczna

Synagoga
Remuh

115

Al. Igr

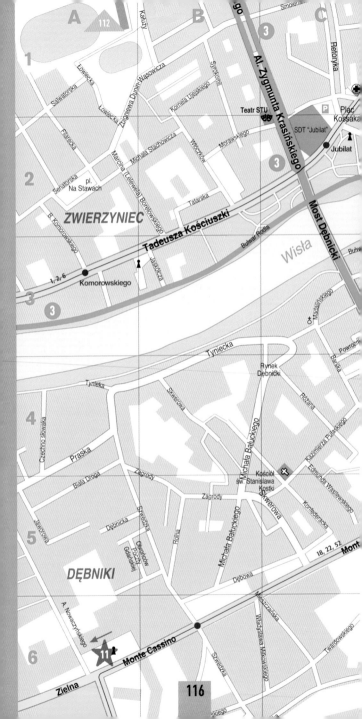

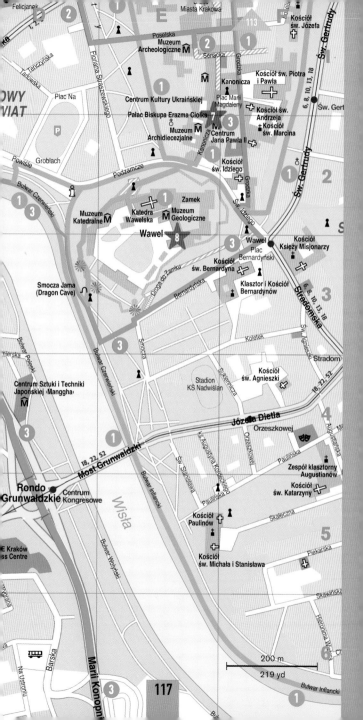

Felicjanek

Miasta Krakowa

Kościół
św. Józefa

Poselska
Muzeum
Archeologiczne

Senacka

Grodzka

113

Floriana Straszewskiego

Tenczyńska

Tarłowska

Plac Na

Centrum Kultury Ukraińskiej

Kanonicza

Plac Marii
Magdaleny

Kościół św. Piotra
i Pawła

Kościół św.
Andrzeja

Kościół
św. Marcina

Pałac Biskupa Erazma Ciołka

Muzeum
Archidiecezjalne

Centrum
Jana Pawła II

Kościół
św. Idziego

Powiśle

Groblach

Podzamcze

Kanonicza

Grodzka

Sw. Gert

Bulwar Czerwieński

Muzeum
Katedralne

Katedra
Wawelska

Zamek

Muzeum
Geologiczne

Wawel

Kościół
Księży Misjonarzy

Wawel
Plac
Bernardyński

Kościół
św. Bernardyna

Smocza Jama
(Dragon Cave)

Droga do Zamku

Bernardyńska

Klasztor i Kościół
Bernardynów

Smocza

Koletek

Stradomska

Stradom

thierska

Bulwar Poleski

Centrum Sztuki i Techniki
Japońskiej ›Manggha‹

Bulwar Czerwieński

Sukiennicza

Stadion
KS Nadwiślan

Kościół
św. Agnieszki

św. Agnieszki

18, 22, 52

Józefa Dietla

Orzeszkowej

Augustiańska

Most Grunwaldzki

18, 22, 52

Orzeszkowej

Paulińska

Zespół klasztorny
Augustianów

Rondo
Grunwaldzkie

Centrum
Kongresowe

Bulwar Inflancki

Ks. Augustyna Kordeckiego

Św. Stanisława

Paulińska

Kościół
św. Katarzyny

Kraków
ss Centre

Kościół
Paulinów

Skałeczna

Wisła

Bulwar Wołyński

Kościół
św. Michała i Stanisława

Piekarska

Skawińska

Hieronima

200 m

219 yd

Barska

Na Ustroniu

Marii Konopni

Bulwar Inflancki

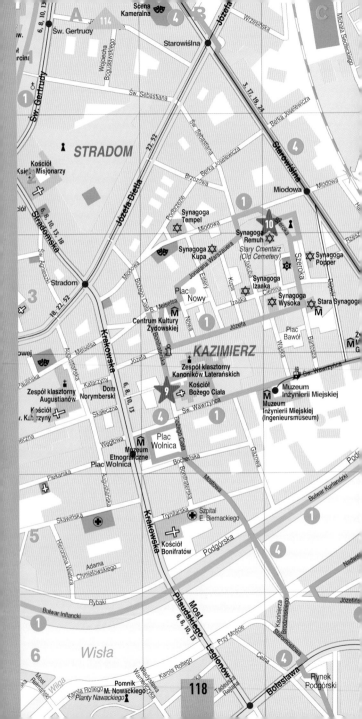

Scéna Kameralna

Św. Gertrudy

Starowiślna

Wrześińska

STRADOM

Kościół Księży Misjonarzy

Stradom

Miodowa

Synagoga Tempel

Synagoga Remuh

Synagoga Kupa

Stary Cmentarz (Old Cemetery)

Synagoga Popper

Plac Nowy

Synagoga Izaaka

Synagoga Wysoka

Stara Synagoga

Centrum Kultury Żydowskiej

KAZIMIERZ

Plac Bawół

Zespół klasztorny Kanoników Laterańskich

Zespół klasztorny Augustianów

Dom Norymberski

Kościół Bożego Ciała

Muzeum Inżynierii Miejskiej

Kościół św. Katarzyny

Muzeum Inżynierii Miejskiej (Ingenieursmuseum)

Muzeum Etnograficzne Plac Wolnica

Plac Wolnica

Szpital E. Biernackiego

Kościół Bonifratów

Podgórska

Bulwar Kurlandzki

Most Piłsudskiego

Legionów

Wisła

Bulwar Inflancki

Pomnik M. Nowackiego *Planty Nawackiego*

118

Bolesława

Rynek Podgórski

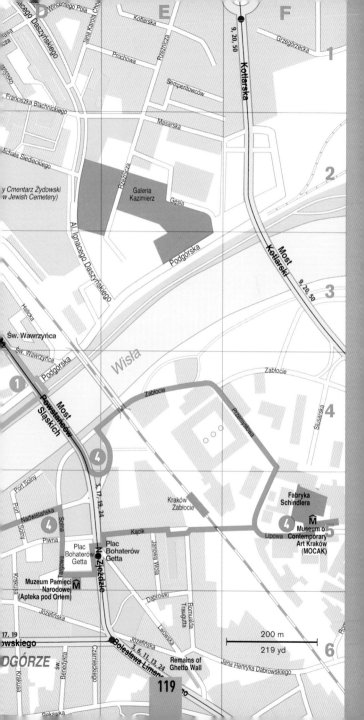

KRAKÓW

WITKOWICE

ZESŁAWICE

NOWA HUTA

Kopiec Wandy

Collegium Maius

ościół Mariacki

Kazimierz

Wawel

RYBITWY

Kopiec Krakusa

PROKOCIM

BIEŻANÓW

Bieżanów

KOSOCICE

Kokotów

Czarnochowice

K. Wielicka

Łagiewniki

Zabawa

OSZOWICE

SOBONIOWICE

Wieliczka

Kopalnia soli

Lasowice

Grabówki

Zbydniowice

Sygneczów

Siercza

Rożnowa

Stoczki

Zdziesławice

Pielgrzymowice

Pustki

Maciejowice

Wiktorowice

Młodziejowice

Książniczki

Boleń

Prawda

Baranów

Czekaj

Bosutów

Kończyce

Zastów

Dłubnia

Węgrzce

Dziekanowice

Raciborowice

Bibice

Batowice

2021

Prusy

776

S7

Drwina Długa

Du Grol

2

4

3

5

1

2

3

4

5

6

8

10

6

6

6

3

3

5

7

5

5

3

2

121

Zachariaszewska

Stare

This index lists a selection of the streets and squares shown in the street atlas

M̂	Museum
😷	Stage / Bühne
ⓘ	Information
✝	Church / Kirche
⚱	Chapel, monastery / Kapelle, Kloster
✡	Synagogue / Synagoge
⊕	Hospital / Krankenhaus
✪	Police / Polizei
🚌	Bus station / Busbahnhof
♟	Monument / Denkmal
P	Parking garage / Parkgarage
⚠	Youth Hostel / Jugendherberge
⟋⟍	Consulate / Konsulat
―●―	Tram with station / Tram mit Station
▪	Remarkable building / Bemerkenswertes Gebäude
▪	Public building / Öffentliches Gebäude
▫	Green / Grünfläche
▫	Uncovered area / Unbebaute Fläche
⧄⧄⧄	Pedestrian zone / Fußgängerzone
▬▬	MARCO POLO Discovery Tour 1 MARCO POLO Erlebnistour 1
▬ ▬	MARCO POLO Discovery Tours MARCO POLO Erlebnistouren
★1	Marco Polo Highlights

INDEX

This index lists all sights, museums, and destinations, plus the names of important people and key words featured in this guide. Numbers in bold indicate a main entry

WRITE TO US

e-mail: sales@heartwoodpublishing.co.uk

Did you have a great holiday? Is there something on your mind? Whatever it is, let us know! Whether you want to praise, alert us to errors or give us a personal tip – MARCO POLO would be pleased to hear from you.

We do everything we can to provide the very latest information for your trip.Nevertheless, despite all of our authors' thorough research, errors can creep in. MARCO POLO does not accept any ability for this. Please contact us by e-mail.

PICTURE CREDITS
Cover photography: Saints Peter and Paul Church (Look/age fotostock)
Photos: R. Freyer (9, 94, 94/95); Getty Images: A. Bizon (19 bottom), M. Dimitrov (3), K. Dydynski (59, 65); Getty Images/EyeEm: N. Kontselidze (68/69); Getty Images/traumlichtfabrik (4 top, 26/27); Laif: D. Biskup (18 top), Geilert/Gaff (97), P. Hirth (6, 14/15, 47, 52/53, 66/67, 73, 76, 82/83), G. Westrich (front flap left, 80), Laif/hemis. fr: J.-D. Sudres (56 right); Laif/Robert Harding Productions/robertharding (60/61); Look: K. Maeritz (45, 54, 70), T. Stankiewicz (34/35); Look/age fotostock (1 top, 8, 12/13, 22, 25, 98 bottom); K. Maeritz (front flap right, 11, 30, 37, 38, 40, 62); Massolit Books: M. Kraft (18 bottom); mauritius images: A. Cupak (20/21); mauritius images/AA World Travel Library/Alamy (49, 95); mauritius images/age: M. Larys (43); mauritius images/Alamy (7, 74/75, 98 bottom, 99), © Bill Bachmann (2), J. Ellis (18 M.), D. Gora (88), M. Kanning (79), T. Pile (110/111), P. Quayle (19 top), S. Reddy (4 bottom, 56 left); J. Ritterbach (16, 50/51), W. Skrypczak (10); mauritius images/Digital-Fotofusion Gallery/Alamy (32); mauritius images/les polders/Alamy (5, 92); Transit-Archiv: Hirth (96, 96/97)

3rd edition 2020 – fully revised and updated
Worldwide distribution: Marco Polo Travel Publishing Ltd, Pinewood, Chineham Business Park, Crockford Lane, Basingstoke, Hampshire RG24 8AL, United Kingdom. Email: sales@marcopolouk.com
© MAIRDUMONT GmbH & Co. KG, Ostfildern
Author: Joanna Tumielewicz; editor: Jens Bey
Picture editor: Stefanie Wiese; What's hot: Joanna Tumielewicz, wunder media, Munich
Cartography street atlas & pull-out map: DuMont Reisekartografie, Fürstenfeldbruck; © MAIRDUMONT, Ostfildern
Design: milchhof : atelier, Berlin; design front cover, pull-out map cover, page 1: factor product Munich; design Discovery Tours, page 2/3: Susan Chaaban Dipl.-Des. (FH)
Translated from German by Robert Scott McInnes, Jane Riester and Rotkel Textwerkstatt e. K., Berlin; editors of the English edition: Rebekah Smith, Marlis von Hessert-Fraatz and Rotkel Textwerkstatt e. K., Berlin
Prepress: Rotkel Textwerkstatt, Berlin
Phrase book in cooperation with Ernst Klett Sprachen GmbH, Stuttgart,
Editorial by Pons Wörterbücher

DOS & DON'TS 👆

A few things you should bear in mind in Krakow

DON'T DRINK ALCOHOL IN PUBLIC OR LITTER THE STREETS

In Poland, it is forbidden to drink alcohol in public and to smoke at public transport stops. Krakow is a clean city and there are rubbish bins on every corner. You will be fined if you are caught throwing away a cigarette butt.

DON'T PARK ILLEGALLY

Krakow is divided into three parking zones and you can only park in Zones B and C if you have a valid parking ticket. If you park your car illegally or without a ticket a wheel clamp will make it impossible for you to drive away – and it will be very expensive to have it removed!

DON'T EXCHANGE MONEY AT THE AIRPORT

The exchange rate at the airport is usually the worst in Krakow; compare the rates in the exchange offices in the city. The rate is usually a few *złoty* lower on Sundays.

DON'T GO INTO A CHURCH INAPPROPRIATELY DRESSED

Being a tourist is no excuse for not observing the rule of not wearing shorts or sleeveless garments when you visit a church. You will either not be allowed to enter or asked to put something on. Some churches, such as St Mary's, will provide you with a shawl. Don't forget to take off your headgear!

DON'T BE CARELESS

Krakow is a safe city but you should still not leave any valuables in your car or your camera on a table in a café. The better hotels have safes for your use.

DON'T GRIPE

The people of Krakow know that things are still not perfect, that the roads could be better, that the pavements need to be repaired and that more cycle paths would be good. The Poles like to grouse themselves but do not take kindly to criticism from foreigners. Concentrate on all the positive things you experience.

DON'T CROSS THE ROAD WITHOUT LOOKING

You should always look to the left and right a few times even if you are at a zebra crossing or traffic light. Drivers do not always stop even if there is a pedestrian by the roadside. Of course, it is compulsory to stop in Poland – but it does not happen very often!

DON'T MAKE JOKES ABOUT THE CHURCH

Around 98 per cent of the Poles are Roman Catholic, and the church still plays a major role in society. Therefore, even if the locals make jokes about priests and the church, you should resist any temptation to do the same.